BUSES ANNUAL

Buses Annual 1974

Edited by GAVIN BOOTH

LONDON
IAN ALLAN LTD

First published 1973

ISBN 07110 0467 6

*Published by Ian Allan Ltd., Shepperton,
Surrey, and printed in the United Kingdom
by Morrison and Gibb Ltd., Edinburgh*

Contents

Preceding pages: Coventry Corporation East Lancs-bodied Daimler Fleetlines in Broadgate. See T. W. Moore's "Coventry Camera" on page 118.

Introduction

The happy inspiration to operate a preserved 1930 AEC Regent on a special London Transport sightseeing route—the cover photograph shows ST922 at Horse Guards Avenue in 1972—resulted in a pleasant blend of the old and the new. *Buses Annual 1974* sets out to capture that same flavour.

The main articles cover the past fifty years, decade by decade. Charles F. Klapper starts off with some memories of developments in the 1920s, and Gortonian follows up with a characteristic description of youthful journeys to Yorkshire in the 1930s. John Parke covers the 1940s with reminiscences of operations in the south-east England, and I allow myself a wallow in nostalgia with some personal notes from the 1950s. To bring the story up to date, Tony Francis describes some of the new thinking which has been typical of certain sections of the bus industry in the 1960s and 1970s.

There are articles on the Isle of Man and on London Transport's vehicle policy, and a wide-ranging article on the history and future of preservation, while Robert E. Jowitt's contribution this year covers two popular pursuits in "Buses and Birds".

In addition to historical coverage, we also strive for a good geographical balance, and many of the best-known photographers have contributed photo-features in our attempt to maintain this.

Here then is *Buses Annual*. I hope that our blend for 1974 includes something to your taste.

Gavin Booth
Edinburgh

The Roaring Twenties

CHARLES F. KLAPPER, FCIT, FRGS, recalls an exciting decade

A Great Western Railway Gilford on the Cheltenham-Oxford limited stop service that was co-ordinated with the trains.

The nascent motor bus industry was badly mauled by World War 1. Motor vehicles and particularly buses were requisitioned by the score, especially if they were of types favoured by the Army. Some bus companies were left only with their Tilling-Stevens petrol-electrics, which the military thought were too complicated to maintain in the field. In general Authority with a Capital A was railway-orientated and unhelpful to the operators of road vehicles, even where workers were being carried to and from munition factories. In 1917 a freeze on service development and severe restrictions on fuel supplies caused wholesale cuts in services as the German submarine campaign against our shipping played havoc with oil imports.

Government failure to appreciate the growing importance of the motor vehicle produced tragic gaps in communication where operators had been unable to maintain pre-war connections; from the drafting of the Railways Act of 1921 the newly founded Ministry of Transport also completely under-estimated the part the road vehicle would play in upsetting the economics of the railways. In the meantime there were some new consolidations of operators such as East Kent and Southdown designed to effect make-do-and-mend on formerly separate and unworkable fleets, while others, such as Ortona of Cambridge and City of Oxford Electric Tramways (which had been spurred by a motor and cycle dealer, William Morris, into providing motor buses instead of the ancient horse tram system) had purchased goods chassis unwanted by the Army and were running double-deck bus bodies mounted on McCurd and $2\frac{1}{2}$-ton Austin vehicles.

Recovery from wartime conditions during 1919 was swift and expansion of the bus industry soon resumed its course. Towards the end of that year the National Steam Car Company decided to give up London operation for three good reasons—the small margin derived from working under London General direction; the soaring cost of fuel, which had gone up 2700%; and the high cost of labour on concession of the eight-hour day. Provincial development seemed to offer more

enticing prospects and by turning to petrol-engined vehicles the company would avoid the stigma police authorities seemed to associate with high-pressure flash boilers. The company had a nucleus of services at Chelmsford, acquired in 1913 from the Great Eastern Railway; it now bought the London General company's Bedford garage as a new centre for expansion. The LGOC had obtained this depot almost by accident in the course of buying the New Central company's business and had tried to sell it in 1913 to the British Electric Traction group. Theodore Thomas once told me that when he was still with the Underground group he tried to sell it to Sydney Garcke, but in 1913 Garcke was still feeling sore at the Tramways (MET) buses having to go on the London streets at General direction and did not want to know about Bedford. The General was glad by 1919 to get rid of an embarrassment (which contravened its articles of association as well as its agreements with other operators) and the National was glad of a chance of growth.

Naturally National began with groups of services round Bedford—to Luton, Cranfield, St Neots, Kimbolton, Biggleswade and Hitchin—while the long-established Great Eastern Railway routes from Chelmsford to Leaden Roding, Good Easter, Great Baddow and Stock were developed to serve Bishops Stortford, Maldon, Billericay and so on. Colchester was also in obvious need of facilities to connect it with Nayland, Sudbury, Harwich and Halstead.

After this the company made lightning progress in opening garages at 55 places in seven years, covering the country from Stroud in Gloucestershire to Swanage on the Dorset coast and right down to Lands End. Many businesses were purchased—the cost was over £282,000 in 1927 alone—including Road Motors of Luton, the Weymouth Motor Company, Hardy Colwills, Devon Motor Transport and its allied Cornwall Motor Transport. By 1927 the fleet numbered 732 and the capital had risen from £300,000 in 1917 to £800,000, of which half was in 7% cumulative preference shares. It is true that on the ordinary shares three lean years followed the 8% of 1920; the reward of 10% for three years then came, with 11¼% in 1927. Two years later railway investment began and National became a holding company, with Western, Southern and Eastern National bus operating concerns. When the Tilling group bought them in 1931 it paid 43s (£2.15) for each £1 National ordinary share. From 1921 onwards National engaged as agent for the London General company in the northern fringes of the Metropolis, and 34 National buses were accordingly licensed in the Metropolitan Police District in 1927. Some of these additions to the fleet were by acquisition rather than expansion and the services of Harvey & Burrows (Hertford & District) which were purchased by the LGOC and transferred to National for operation were a case in point.

United Automobile Services was another swiftly expanding company in the 1920s. It began modestly enough with four buses at Lowestoft in 1912, but before the year was out four more had begun work from Bishop Auckland in County Durham. The original operation spread from Suffolk to Norfolk and South Lincolnshire and at the end of 1919 there were 64 buses in the fleet. A few months later Len Balls, almost singlehanded, was opening garages in industrial south-east Northumberland. In 1922 UAS buses reached Ripon in Yorkshire and in 1926 the headquarters were transferred to York as a central point between Berwick and Southwold, although no operation took place there. Before a still greater growth took place through railway investment and the transfer of half the shares to Tilling & British Automobile Traction, the fleet of four had grown to 619 by 1928 and the capital of £9,000 to £460,000.

In 1931, after the company had become responsible for operating London & North Eastern Railway buses in County Durham

National Omnibus and Transport FCX type Guy
followed by 40-seat AEC at Bedford.

A private hire in a fleet of United Automobile
Services Bristols at Scarborough in the late 1920s.

RIVIER
3
UNITED
L
77
VF-5177

and many railway purchases, such as Robert Emerson & Co. Ltd, running between Newcastle and Carlisle or Blumer's Bus Service serving Middlesbrough and Hartlepool, it was decided that the local nature of omnibus supervision called for rationalisation. The East Anglian business was therefore ceded to a new Eastern Counties Omnibus Company, which also took in Ortona, Peterborough Electric Traction, and the Tilling-founded Eastern Counties Road Car concern. UAS services in Parts of Holland were sold to Lincolnshire Road Car for £23,000. Transfer of the headquarters to Darlington then seemed a logical step.

If you have a feeling that there is something abitrary about bus timetabling, you are probably right. In general the areas where services were initiated by National have much sparser services today than those of United or, still more strikingly, those begun by Cannon and Mackenzie, either in Southdown or in their Wilts & Dorset venture. The National direction, inspired by Walter James Iden, well known as the planner of the mass production of the B-type bus at Walthamstow, tended to economise on vehicle-mileage and to provide market-day and shopping services on certain days rather than regular headway facilities all through the week. Although United Automobile did not begin the day's work in time for the commuter they very often then provided an hourly headway from mid-morning to well into the evening. On Southdown routes the regular headway was in operation at an early date; from Brighton to Eastbourne, for example, nearly all the buses left at 10 past the hour by 1924; by that time the Brighton to Portsmouth service was already half-hourly from 0945 to 1645 and many others were beginning to assume their close-headway nature as Douglas Mackenzie made use of his discovery that if a bus every two hours was unsatisfactory, one every 30 minutes would often "bring them off their bicycles", as he used to put it.

So it is in these early years of the 1920s that one can see the patterns of today taking shape, giving us regular headways daily from Margate through the South of England as far

west as Shaftesbury and north of London into the industrial Midlands and the North of England, but with more irregular operation in East Anglia, the West Country, and North and Central Wales. Much of this is dictated by thin population, but some of it because from the earliest days of the country motor bus the locals have never had a chance of using a bus every day of the week at regular headways. One or two endeavours to restore or create such facilities since the war have failed because by then use of personal transport had become habitual.

The acme of National economy was probably some time in the rush of the company's expansion in Dorset, when it was discovered that a service had been taken off for lack of custom after three days' running, the day before the appropriate department got round to distributing the handbills to advertise it.

Roaring competition prevailed during the decade beginning in 1921. The Chocolate Express Leyland of Arthur George Partridge restarted it in London on August 5, 1922; the Tilling traffic manager, Harry Webb, had been into the Leyland New Kent Road shops the previous night, so that when Partridge left the garage two General chasers were fully equipped with the same route and fare boards as the Express and were never at a loss as he changed from 19 (where Partridge, as a prewar busman, had felt pity for the long postwar queues from Clapham Junction in the morning) to 11 and to 33 for a run to Richmond in the evening and on Sundays. Eventually over 500 independent buses were running in London and the LGOC and its associates sought redress by legislation rather than by physical tactics, although these were meted out to the end to Percy Frost-Smith's petrol-electric vehicles, but then he had been Tilling's engineer.

London was not unique; a hoard of small operators, some with over-bodied Ford Model T's, ran between Slough and Windsor; there were 200 buses owned by 55 different operators jostling for business with the Potteries Electric Traction Company, which was popular with the local council neither for its trams nor its buses and almost any applicant could get a licence from Stoke-on-Trent Corporation to compete with the establishment. Competition was often most rife where no strong operating company was concerned, or round a boundary town where two established operators met. Independents thus seethed round Newbury in Berkshire and Basingstoke in Hampshire; they were unable to get a similar footing in towns where close control of public transport was carried out, often though this was purely manipulated for the advantage of the municipal tramway system. Sometimes this could be overcome by issuing return tickets to passengers, so that the bus was not technically "plying for hire" on the return trip. During the 1920s the example of Birmingham Corporation and the Birmingham & Midland Motor Omnibus Co. Ltd, which had made an agreement in 1914 under which the company buses charged a higher protective fare to just beyond the city boundary, was increasingly followed; agreements were usually tailor-made to suit local circumstances and a large company such as Ribble would find it had perhaps 100 agreements with 25 or more local authorities.

As a result the buses of the large area-agreement operators were allowed into the centres of the towns and timetable information such as "Frequent trams from Hazel Grove—or Stockport—to Manchester" gradually could be eliminated. Buses from Manchester to Cheadle were advertised in 1921 to have a running time of 16 min, which looked pretty speedy until one saw that the real bus journey started at Palatine Road tram terminus. The Ribble bus route from Preston to Bolton ended at Horwich tram terminus, although another ran every two hours right through via Westhoughton. From Southport, Ormskirk and St Helens there was an as yet unbridged gap in 1921 to Liverpool. Even municipal buses kept off the tramway grass; in that same

Ortona SOS 37-seat Q-type on Cambridge-Saffron Walden service.

year Wigan Corporation buses to Skelmersdale began from Abbey Lakes tram terminus in Upholland; for Billinge the Wigan bus left the Wigan tramway route at Orrell Post. On the Yorkshire side of the Pennines let the Huddersfield–Dewsbury service suffice as an example. There were trams from Huddersfield to Bradley (and according to timetable compilers trams were always "frequent trams"), a bus service from Bradley to Ravensthorpe, followed by 20 minutes on a tram into the centre of Dewsbury. This was the classic worn-out tramway track where the general manager of the tramways company had to threaten to resign and put on his own bus service to drag his employers into the motor era. To be fair, they had been trying to make a success of the motors since 1913 and only took them off in 1921. Even if that was a mistake, acknowledged by reinstating them on April 12, 1922, the trams for another dozen years handled more passengers than the buses in Dewsbury.

Although competition was fierce I cannot remember in the 1920s any of the outright dangerous tactics that around 1910 had led to actual collisions between rival buses in London, although trying to see a competitor off by running one bus in front and one behind sometimes gave rise to unpleasantness. In London the driver of an ancient General B-type, told by his inspector to go after a competing independent, just said: "Wot, catch a Leyland?" On a Trent route a new competitor was subjected to the usual nursing, and after following him about all the morning the Trent driver went after him into a housing estate, where the rival came to rest outside a private house. The driver then got down out of his cab and as he walked towards the Trent bus turned out to be a giant of burly and truculent appearance. To the Trent man's relief, when the nursed one gave tongue, it was to say: "Tha's been following me all morning; wouldsta like bite of dinner wi' me?" And they had a little jolly over hotpot and a glass of beer before resuming serious competition in the afternoon.

In the Spring of 1921 Charles E. Lee was organising the *Travel by Road Guide*, which he edited for the first four issues; looking at those early issues today one is struck by the sparsity of some services which, despite erosion from the private car, do better today. Nostalgically one remembers many names which half a century ago were meaningful in the bus business. The Isle of Sheppey scored a first in the league for abandoning electric tramways, when the Sheerness & District Electric Power & Traction gave up in 1917 and the Standen family took over with Sheppey Motor Transport buses. In 1921 they operated between Sheerness, Queenborough, Eastchurch and Sittingbourne, a peculiar feature being the very small number of journeys worked before noon. Carey Brothers of New Romney offered daily journeys (one each way) to Folkestone and market facilities to Ashford and Rye with the proviso "Services increased in summer as traffic demands." There were still sturdy country carriers like Bulmer who did a round from Faversham through Otterden to Ashford and Istead who linked Hurstmonceux with Hailsham, with projections to Lewes.

Autocar Services had been established in and around Tunbridge Wells since 1909; Redcar lashed the establishment with competition from 1923 for a decade, some of the services being the same but with short extensions; Ashby was another competitor, who lasted for two years or so only. Autocar itself had ambitions for other operators' green fields and in 1920 worked to Farnborough to meet London buses—right across territory claimed by East Surrey and taken up by them in 1922 with the East Surrey purchase of the Dartford–Farningham route pioneered by W. P. Allen. East Surrey in 1921 ceased to be orientated on Reigate and operated services radially from London suburban centres; in 1932 it became London General Country Services and took over services from a number of London General agents, including National, and others ranging from the Great Western Railway to Autocar Services. This was preparatory to the formation of the London Passenger Transport Board; today these services are controlled by the National Bus Company through London Country, after over 35 years of working by LPTB and its successors, as the Country Department of London Transport.

In Hampshire the Newbury & Andover Motor Co Ltd, with a three-times-daily service on Monday, Tuesday and Wednesday, twice on Sunday, and a two-hourly headway on Thursday, Friday, Saturday, gained a lot of publicity at its 1920 start by serving an ex-servicemen's home en route. An operator I well remember for its primrose yellow fleet was Mobility Ltd; most of its operations were between Andover, Bullington, Sutton Scotney and Winchester and between Andover, Whitchurch and Basingstoke. From Meonstoke Meon Valley Motor Service ran by three routes to Winchester on various days and on Monday went down to Fareham market. Round Weymouth the railway buses were Great Western and London & South Western Joint. The LSWR was still running once each way between Chagford and Exeter on four days a week and the GWR worked from Chagford to Moretonhampstead Station six journeys every weekday.

Coming back to the Home Counties, the Aylesbury Motor Bus Company was well established, but the Amersham & District's two short routes gave little hint that it might become of interest to the London General. The United Counties Omnibus & Road Transport Company was in September, 1921, to take over the Wellingborough Motor Omnibus Co Ltd, founded eight years before; in 1928 it acquired the business of the Northampton Motor Omnibus Co Ltd. Other Northampton operators of 1921 were F & E Beeden and the Midland Motor Bus Co Ltd.

James Fryer Ltd formed Hereford Transport in 1920 and by the following year there were a dozen services established. At first mainly on the south of the city, services embraced the Leominster and Ludlow areas by 1924 and were absorbed in the rapidly expanding Red & White group two years

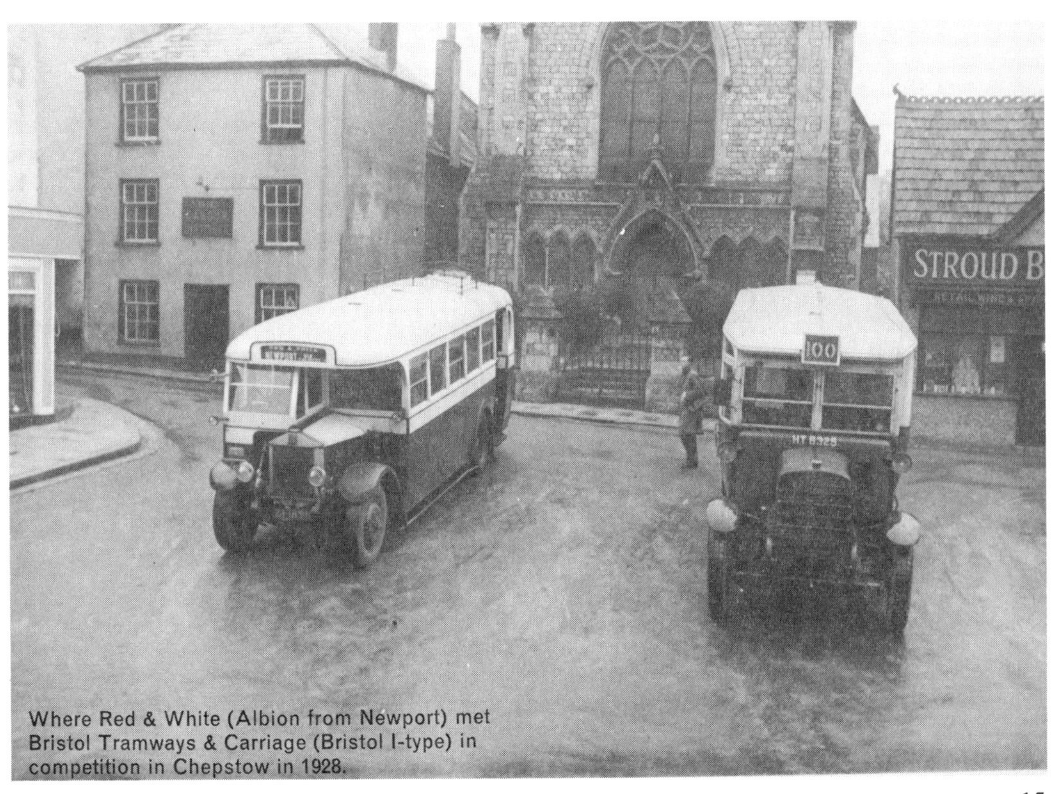

Where Red & White (Albion from Newport) met Bristol Tramways & Carriage (Bristol I-type) in competition in Chepstow in 1928.

later. Radiating from Tenbury were the infrequent services of the curiously named Tenbury Baths Co Ltd. What is now East Midland territory was administered as Clowne & District. For that matter it was still a few years before Barnsley & District was to change its name to Yorkshire Traction. Until April, 1923, what became the North Western Road Car Co Ltd was operating as the Macclesfield, Stockport and Buxton districts of British Automobile Traction Co Ltd; the new concern took in the Mid-Cheshire Motor Bus Co Ltd of Northwich, with half a dozen or so services, in November, 1924, and Altrincham District at the beginning of 1926. In 1921 Barrow–Ulverston was still served by British Automobile Traction buses.

A book could be written on the changes in operating pattern in Lincolnshire. W. T. Underwood Ltd, was formed as a United Automobile subsidiary in 1920 and became East Midland in 1927. Lincolnshire Road Car sprang in 1928 from the Silver Queen services based on Lincoln. The Lincolnshire business of East Midland at Scunthorpe and Froding-ham was, however, transferred in the mid-summer of 1927 to Enterprise & Silver Dawn Motors, which also absorbed Progressive Motor Omnibus of Boston.

Llandudno was another centre of competi-tion—with North Wales Silver Motors, Llandudno Motor & Garage Co (Red Garages), which ran the Royal Red buses, and Llandudno Coaching & Carriage Com-pany, with the Royal Blue fleet. The last-mentioned was a horse concern registered in 1897, which had been the subject of British Automobile Traction investment; as a con-sequence a good proportion of the fleet was built by Birmingham & Midland Motor Omnibus Co Ltd, as were Ortonas, Peter-boroughs and Northern Generals, as well as some moiety of the Trent and Potteries fleets.

Nostalgic names as one flicks through the *TBR* guide include South Wales Commercial Motors, Lydney & Dean Forest, Tocia (Pwllheli), Nevin & District, New Quay Road Motor Service, Lake District Road Traffic Company, and the always imposing Ullswater Royal Mail Service; some of these

disappeared under the stress of competition.

The effect of competition, no matter how often it led to expansion of business through the principle of "facilities begetting traffic", no matter how colourful and interesting rival activities on the roads might appear, was always the same—that unregulated competi-tion produced bankruptcy, consolidation, poorer services and less attractive conditions of employment for the staff concerned. In London, through the swift blast of the independent bus invasion of the hitherto immune company tramway routes, labour troubles on the tramways conspired to per-suade Parliament to pass the London Traffic Act, 1924, which paved the way—after some injustices and some quite stupid police dictatorship, including an impracticable ser-vice numbering system—to the London Passenger Transport Board monopoly nine years later. For the country in general the need to curb unregulated competition gave rise to the Road Traffic Act, 1930, by which a much-needed licensing system was set up and the hours of busmen were controlled. Although the Traffic Commissioners made many mistakes when they were learning how to do their job the eventual effect was a strong industry which had great flexibility for providing the public with the services it required and was a vast improvement over the patchy local regulation which had formerly prevailed, and which in more than one instance provided cases of conflicting technical requirements between towns naturally joined by one bus service, but where the buses could not run through without defying the law at one end or the other.

And so the roaring twenties gave place to the well-regulated expansion of the thirties, but not without some qualms and some sad losses of some of the operators who had played vital roles in the progress of the motor bus network of this country—providing a more comprehensive network than any other country in Europe has enjoyed and a far better one than the early rise of the private car and the late development of the road system have ever permitted in the United States.

Peaceful Demonstrations

An earlier demonstrator, Crossley Condor RG 1676, on loan to Nottingham Corporation in 1932.

281 ATC, the prototype Leyland Atlantean with Metro-Cammell body, on loan to Potteries in 1957.

Above: Leyland/MCW Olympic HR40 KOC 241 on a proving run in 1951.

Right: Another early underfloor-engined integral demonstrator, AEC/Park Royal Monocoach NLP 635, photographed in 1953 while in service with London Transport at Reigate.

Guy Arab UF demonstrator LJW 336, with Saro body, on Newcastle's Tyne Bridge on hire to Northern General.

A more exotic location, Ford R192
demonstrator JOO 674C with
Duple body, on a test trip in the
Caucasus.

On demonstration work during the
1957 Scottish Motor Show, a Guy
Warrior with Willowbrook bus body.

Over the Ups and in the Downs

GORTONIAN remembers youthful forays across the Pennines

Bradford Corporation was a confirmed AEC user. Bus 430 is here pictured in Leeds at the City Square terminus.

Our Editor asked me a little while ago if I would provide him with an article which would illustrate some facets of the passenger transport industry as operating within the West Riding of Yorkshire in the immediate prewar years.

It then occurred to me that my journeys fell into two parts hence the rather odd title, namely the actual process of travelling across and over the Pennines from the Lancashire side, and then taking full note of all that there was to see once in this somewhat alien and certainly very different territory.

I suppose I was lucky because our regular trans-pennine trips followed several different paths, and these took us either into the Halifax/Bradford area, or to Leeds via Huddersfield, or else into the southern part of the county when we would visit Pontefract or Doncaster, and it really was surprising how the whole character of the various local operators policy with regard to the running of their undertakings and/or their particular vehicles could vary.

As it is obvious from the preceeding paragraph that our lines of communication were well defined I propose to deal with each of them in turn, on this two part basis, commencing with the more northerly routes, which led us towards Halifax and Bradford.

The easiest way to reach Halifax from home was to pick up one of the two express services which then ran through Oldham and were worked either by Yorkshire Woollen District and North Western Road Car Company on a joint basis or the erstwhile Ripponden & District Motors Limited that provided some highly competitive facilities, for approximately one decade.

The Oldham–Halifax route had been pioneered by North Western in April 1926 but on April 15, 1927, Oldham Corporation also appeared when a 90-minute frequency was introduced. The Corporation used their single-deck Leyland one-man operated normal control machines (nine in number) and charged a single fare of 1s 8d or 3s return with a minimum fare out of Oldham of 7d, which took one as far as the Rams Head, a public house high on the moors above Denshaw.

From that point to Derby Bar the Lancashire or West Riding milestones marked the stage points and then there was another minimum fare of 5d that gave protection to the Halifax trams—to be mentioned later—from Kebroyd to the town centre.

By 1928 the undertaking's brown Karrier or Guy single-deckers were also being used and application was made to the various local councils for licences to allow some of its double-deckers of similar make and fearsome aspect to help out at peak periods, but alas the Lancashire municipality fell foul of the Wakefield-based West Riding County authorities who took out an injunction alleging damage to roads and so Oldham operations came to an end on July 28, 1928, when the BET companies were left with but a single competitor, and in order to offset his activities they projected their route into Manchester from Oldham on May 15, 1929.

Ripponden & District had started as a purely local concern in 1921 when a link was provided between that village and the Halifax trams at the Triangle, but in 1925 expanded to give a thrice daily service from Sowerby Bridge to Oldham, but before long a fourth trip was added which left Sowerby Bridge at 10.35 am and was extended through to Manchester on Tuesday and Thursdays only. This bus route rather uniquely shared its terminal points with a waterway as both the Sowerby Bridge and Manchester stands were on the terminal properties of the Rochdale Canal Company.

Because of the difficulty in obtaining licences from a very unfriendly Halifax the Horton Street/Wards End Royal Oak yard was also rented and so from this further piece of private property it was possible to work on the return ticket system between Halifax and Manchester every two hours from April 15, 1927. Traffic grew apace and so on March 25, 1929, the frequency was increased to one bus every sixty minutes and these were simultaneously projected back from Halifax to Shelf which is of course on the edge of Bradford, that city being reached on April 4, 1930, but again a ride outwards was only possible if you held a return ticket.

By the latter date Ripponden were working a loosely co-ordinated service with Halifax Corporation from Cunning Corner through Rishworth, Ripponden and Sowerby Bridge to Halifax, which was introduced in March 1928 and also on its own account from Sowerby Bridge to Ripponden via Mill Bank and the Beehive, a section possessing steep gradients, narrow roads and not over much traffic. These workings began on March 4, 1927, to Mill Bank only where most buses still reversed. The Ripponden extension, which dated from November 1929, was intended for shoppers and was restricted to Friday and Saturday evenings. Other Ripponden routes ran from Ripponden to Rishworth (Commons) opened as late as July 1933 and finally from Ripponden to Elland. The latter gave connectional facilities in Ripponden with the buses to or from Manchester, and from July 31, 1929, was extended from Elland over Elland Bridge to Wakefield Road

and thence Brighouse. Incidentally Halifax Corporation had reached Rishworth and Cunning Corner on October 1, 1928, following a successful bid for the Ryburn bus business.

The Ripponden concern showed every initiative in developing its business, and one of the freely distributed neat folded and glazed card pocket timetables, still in my possession, shows that in the peak years buses left the Dale Street, Rochdale Canal Yard, Manchester, almost at the foot of London Road (or Piccadilly) Station approach, at 8.30 am and then every hour until 8.30 pm with two later buses at 9.30 pm and 10.30 pm going to Halifax only.

You paid the 5s 6d return fare, boarded one of the smart blue/cream single-deckers and travelled outwards via Bristow Lane to Newton Heath and Oldham, which was reached in 22 minutes. There the buses called at Rhodes Bank before climbing up through Grains Bar to reach the Yorkshire boundary

This shot typifies the sort of rolling stock—double- and single-deck—used by North Western around Oldham from about 1936 until after the War. 934, which had an ECOC body, was new in 1938 and lasted in the form shown until 1953/4 when it was rebodied and renumbered 670.

and the moorland section. Operating difficulties over the 1,000 ft contour were particularly severe in winter but the older inhabitants still remember the strenuous efforts made by the company to dig the roads clear after snowfalls.

Bradford was reached in a little under two hours and the return times from the Packard Garage on Thornton Road were similar to those from Manchester namely thirty minutes past the hour from 6.30 am to 8.30 pm with two later services being provided on Saturdays and Sundays. This sort of late running was quite general in prewar days and one can only assume that the populous was then very active socially.

Ripponden had a most up to date fleet mainly of Leyland or AEC manufacture but the outstanding vehicles were two all-Leyland double-deckers (one with an oil engine) and a Leyland Lioness that commenced life with an angular body but was later to be rebuilt to something that can only be described as "streamline in excelcis".

The poor old Tilling-Stevens of North Western did not have a price, in fact it was a case of the tortoise and the hare, but like the fable the tortoise won in the end for the larger companies objected to the Ripponden application for a Bradford–Manchester licence after the introduction of the 1930 Traffic Act and were successful in their endeavours with the result that operations had to be cut back to Halifax as from May 8, 1932. The Ripponden to Brighouse service suffered a similar curtailment to Elland only at the same time for a similar reason and a little over two years later the newly formed Halifax Joint Omnibus Committee took over the local Halifax to Rishworth Commons or Cunning Corner services. Ripponden stage carriage activities lasted until September 1936 when the Joint Omnibus Committee took over the Elland route and the BET Subsidiaries the Manchester timetable to run it *in toto* until November 22 when a rationalisation took place and the former Ripponden workings were amalgamated with those of their new owners.

Ripponden was, of course, the place where our second route from Lancashire came into

the Ryburn Valley but as the journey from Oldham to Halifax, when one used this facility, was just about double in time, mileage and cost over the direct run it was not an excursion that was made over often.

One commenced at Star Inn catching the hourly single-deck express service (no. 7), that since February 22, 1928, had linked Ashton with Rochdale and was in the middle 1930s the stamping ground of Oldham's petrol-engined TS1 machines or their later oil-engined counterparts. These gave a quick ride over the Thornham Summit but if you should miss the bus then an alternative was available through the medium of the no. 7 tramcar which took one to that same Summit on a route which had already been abandoned in favour of buses between Oldham and Summit and trolleybuses between Oldham and Hathershaw (which carried on to Ashton) —and then reinstated. The trams commenced their journey at Hathershaw on the Ashton boundary and so were paralleled throughout the whole length of their track by the express buses. The usual performers in the years immediately prior to closure in November 1937 were the twelve Chamberlain cars of 1928 (Nos 121–132) with fully enclosed fronts and over heavy looking top decks. They had brown leather upholstered seats in both saloons but nevertheless comfort was not one of their strong points, although this aspect of the matter was not helped by the condition of the track which certainly in Royton, with the exception of a single short stretch relaid in 1927 could be described as "somewhat run down".

These cars or their older open balcony sisters, also frequently encountered, could not additionally be accused of being speedy but would finally arrive at Summit after a trip of about 25 minutes, and there one expected to find the Rochdale local conveyance awaiting —although from time to time as the Oldham tram breasted the hill about 300 yards from the end of the track the impatient and anxious traveller was greeted with the sight of the tail end of his connection vanishing northwards.

Until the April of 1931 that connection would have been a tramcar, and I wish I could tell you of its livery but certainly in their later years all such Rochdale rolling stock was arrayed in a nondescript browny black hue that could have been varnished teak, dark brown, pure dirt, or a mixture of all three.

By the middle 1930s though, all this had been swept aside and Rochdale buses were finished in the smart blue/cream that made them outstanding amongst other Manchester area fleets, although I was not amused when someone began to fit blue tinted glass to the front lower saloon bulkhead windows. As this was before the War the only conclusion I could come to was that the sun was particularly strong in that outpost of the British Empire.

Finally, however, Rochdale centre was reached and there came a change on to the single-deck Hebble vehicle, almost certainly of Albion manufacture, that was bound for Halifax and eventually Leeds. Had it not been for the unfortunate attitude of the West Riding County Council already mentioned our bus would have been in Halifax colours.

That municipality started the Rochdale service on August 28, 1926, which it ran initially hourly or towards the end each 90 minutes until June 29, 1927, when it finally retired leaving the field to Rochdale Corporation. That municipality also fell foul of the Wakefield politicians so its stay too was brief, lasting until December 3, 1928, when the LMS railway came on the scene.

This rather unlikely bus owner employed about eight Leyland single-deckers that were in best railway parlance allocated to Rochdale but one stayed overnight in the Halifax goods yards to work the first outwards trip which ran only to Ripponden (Gig Mill) each morning at 5.30 am. The through service ran every 90 minutes from station to station from 7.00 am until 10.00 pm with return times ex Rochdale spanning the period 6.55 am until 9.55 pm.

The setting up of the Halifax Joint Committee and the sale of the then private Hebble company to the LMS and later still in part to the BET brought another re-organisation in its train and so on December 10, 1933, Hebble became the sitting tenants. They stayed until February 22, 1971, when Halifax buses came back once more, but that is all another story which has been dealt with in *Buses* in recent times by John Ryburn. (*Buses* No. 193, April 1971.)

From our point of view the Hebble service had the attraction that it was more frequent than any other crossing the Pennines in this particular region, 30 minute intervals often being provided, but like all Pennine crossings it offered little of interest to the transport enthusiast until one came to more populous parts. For me Triangle was a sort of frontier Mecca; I was a keen tram worshipper and it was at this unlikely spot almost in the middle of nowhere that Halifax tracks began, although the original ambition had been to reach Ripponden and Cunning Corner. Lack of hard municipal cash and the objections of the Lancashire & Yorkshire Railway Company seem to have been the inhibiting factors.

Those tracks were incredibly narrow being set just 3 ft 6 in apart and they carried not portly covered-topped cars but slim chicks entirely devoid of any upper deck protection. Now I can never remember seeing any open-topped tram (apart from the Stockport works vehicle) around Manchester so these seemed like survivors from a mediaeval age, but they could travel at surprising speed along the single track that led down to Sowerby Bridge, and lasted until July 25, 1934, abandonment following 12 months of argument. After Sowerby came an odd loop or two and then from the borough boundary double track all the way into Halifax with a series of junctions at King Cross—alas mostly disused. The domed-roof covered-top trams of quite recent construction ran out to Hebden Bridge and Tuel Lane until 1935 or 1938 respectively, and the Sowerby Bridge trams also came to an end at the same time, November 29, 1938.

In 1934 Halifax had 83 trams which were painted in one of two shades of red, but this colour scheme was quite outshone by that applied to the buses, which then numbered 79. This figure rose to 118 by March 1938 when the trams were down to 38.

My first remembered glimse of the orange/

green/cream mixture came as a petrol-engined single-decker appeared out of a Ryburn Valley mist and my immediate reaction was to say "uggh", but after a time my attitude changed and I was quite attracted to the Glasgow-like combination. I was not too attracted to the bus fleet though, partially because it was taking over from the trams and partially because the Corporation had been standardising on the AEC ever since 1929 when the first ever Regent Mark I MT2114 was borrowed for trial purposes.

Most of the modern stock had Park Royal or Roe bodies and oil engines and the 8.8 litre figured in the double-deckers—and perhaps here was the cause of my attitude. They always seemed rough in comparison to the Leyland or Gardner powered vehicles used in my home area.

Some of the earlier intake of the early 1930s bordered on the archaic as certain double-deckers had open staircases and roofs with a most peculiar contour, but more fetching still were the survivors of the even earlier Karrier era, the last of which finally succumbed in the February of 1934 after a life of just four years and three months. We would see all these and more as we travelled through the Town Centre but after January 9, 1934, there were no trams to be seen on the Bradford side of Halifax, the last section to close being the mile of single track which linked Halifax with Shibden Park Gates and here was a situation I have never been able to understand.

There were and still are two main ways of reaching Bradford from Halifax using roads through Boothtown and Queensbury or Northowram and Shelf.

The former was served after the Queensbury trams were withdrawn on March 31, 1934, by Hebble buses which ran through to Bradford, and had done so to the Corporation's chagrin since the 1926 General Strike, along with Joint Omnibus Committee vehicles which went to Queensbury itself, plus Halifax Corporation trams—or buses from August 5, 1934—which ran almost to the borough boundary above Boothtown. This all meant that although there was no Corporation

through service at least the Bradford and Halifax vehicles did meet end on in Queensbury.

Now until August 16, 1932, the position had been duplicated at Shelf, only on that date the trams to Halifax were discontinued and Corporation buses provided but they terminated at Northowram (Queen Victoria). All the track and overhead remained *in situ* though and each day a tram trundled out to Northowram and then began to work a shuttle service from that point to Shelf.

One of the three Halifax single-deck trams was often employed on this duty until March 31, 1933, when the shuttle was finally discontinued, but now there was no Halifax vehicles to Shelf at all for the buses (Corporation not JoC) terminated still at Northowram and Hebble buses reigned supreme on the road thence to Shelf.

Hebble incidentally did not extend the Albion principle to double-deck purchases. Leylands were the choice here and certain choice specimens did their best to outpace the Halifax 8.8's. Generally speaking, fortune seemed to favour Southall but the runs which stick in my mind always involve Hebble buses and the precipitous slopes and curves of the Queensbury to Boothtown section—but that is another road and another story.

At Shelf though things were different for now we were in Bradford territory, and until February 19, 1935, that Corporation's blue-liveried cars terminated in the village, and I must say at the outset that my first encounter as a passenger with a Bradford tram gave me a pleasant surprise. They all looked both alike and Edwardian, having open upper balconies, large route number blinds, and enclosed platforms but their looks belied the comfort aspect for I never travelled on one that did not have quite generously proportioned upholstered seating on either deck. The track too was kept in good condition, and even after the War right up to November 5, 1949, when the route was finally closed, it was possible to ride up and down the fantastic gradient that lay between Bradford and Queensbury and never be jarred by a broken rail joint or a hundred yards or so of mixed corrugations. These trams too could beat the Hebble Leyland going up: downhill the reverse applied.

The express bus would, of course, sweep through Shelf and then came a surprise, for a piece of reserved tramway track came into view. A portion of this, which could not have then been all that old, was abandoned when Shelf operations ceased but the remainder to Odsal was retained until the very last day of the Bradford trams, May 6, 1950, to serve the Horsfall playing fields and the residents of the vicinity—but latterly only a peak hour or Saturday facility was provided.

Another tram route to be mentioned later came in at Odsal as did the single-decked Oakenshaw trolleybus, that died on August 1, 1940, the first to be encountered. Further interest was provided by the Manchester Road depot, and the view a little nearer the City of a double track vanishing off to the right between some mills of standard West Riding appearance to a place which according

to the blinds on the cars was known as Bowling Old Lane, a goal I was later to reach with some disappointment as I had been expecting that the route would be far longer than it actually was.

This route continued until December 13, 1947.

In March 1939, before the outbreak of War, the Bradford fleet consisted of approximately 136 trolleybuses, 104 buses and 135 trams, the last-mentioned making a comeback on September 11, 1939, on to the Undercliffe route from which they had been banished on April 8, 1935. Incredibly both track and overhead had survived for $4\frac{1}{2}$ years because, so I am told, the department could not then afford to reinstate the roads and so took good care to retain the running rights, although by March 1940 the tram fleet was down to 112. I was therefore able to have many more rides on that steeply inclined section and its companion route to Bradford Moor, but there was later a corresponding

Streamline in excelsis. Before being rebodied this Leyland Lion was often employed on the Rippondon to Elland route.

deprivation with the ending of the service beyond Thornbury to Stanningley on October 18, 1942. Much later, but still in the War, came the abandonment of the last long tram service that had run out to Bailiff Bridge, which I will mention in a few more paragraphs, for I was to see this for the first time from yet another express bus—and here we come to our third Pennine highway.

This ran into Yorkshire at Lees, where until 1928 Oldham trams had reversed, but 15 miles further east rails began again at the Marsden terminus of Huddersfield Corporation tramways, a spot we first reached following a picnic that had taken us on to Standege. We walked down the moor into Marsden and there sat in the little park awaiting the bus home—or rather should have sat in the park; I refused to commune with lawns and flowers, my whole attention being taken by a trolley reverser.

No self-respecting Yorkshire tram trailed a trolley rope behind it as did the Lancashire cars. Instead a long bamboo pole was carried on two or three rocker panel hooks, which all seemed bizarre and undesirable to my foreign eyes, but now a reverser . . . well that was something again.

Something else again were the tramcars for this meeting must have taken place around 1932 as every tram that came into view was obviously almost brand new so I began to think that Huddersfield must be a tramway Mecca worthy of the highest devotion—although I was not to know that the cars in the 137 to 144 series were to be the 1932 swansong of the local pro tram faction.

Fortunately from my point of view it was a fine warm evening and so my parents were persuaded to let one bus go to give me more spotting time.

It was just as well as it turned out that our departure suffered this postponement for that conveyance came into violent contact with a heavy lorry on the way down to Diggle and we saw the splintered results of the encounter as we passed in a red/black machine which belonged to the Hanson concern.

Hansons were another private company that gave the establishment a lot of trouble in earlier years and at this time they served the Huddersfield – Marsden – Uppermill – Oldham route upon which they had been established for several years, every 120 minutes using single-deckers of AEC or Albion manufacture. Over most of the 18 miles that separated the two terminals operations were conducted on a limited stop basis but the route was an undoubted boon to the people living up in various moorland hamlets who could and did stop the buses almost anywhere upon request.

Hansons did not have everything to themselves as the bigger concerns also carried a considerable long distance cross-Pennine traffic whilst Oldham Corporation had also designs on Huddersfield passengers in 1928 and had actually fitted certain buses with appropriate destination screens just before the Halifax debacle took place. This event put paid to its West Riding ambitions, but the Corporation faction finally triumphed on October 1, 1969, when Huddersfield buses appeared and Hansons passed into stage carriage history.

Hansons were, in this period, both ambitious and apparently encouraged by certain locals who wished to see an alternative route opened which would travel not via Uppermill but on the slightly shorter road which runs through Delph, and thus provide a second string to the bow.

Such a route was in fact opened around 1936/37 when North Western began operations, that Company working along the main road from Delph Station to the Horse and Jockey where the Uppermill/Lees alternative came in. Although it also involved a two-hour round journey time, the service was not so regular as the Hanson facility, and sad to say not so well used, with the result that before long the initial Tilling-Stevens had been replaced by what was known colloquially as a "flying pig", or in pure technical parlance one of the long-snouted Dennis Ace front-entrance 20-seaters of 1934 that were numbered from 651 to 654 (E.C.W.) and 655/656 (Harrington).

In an attempt to improve patronage the route was diverted to travel through Delph from about 12 months after commencement and the flying pigs departed, to be replaced by other Dennis buses of larger size or Bristols, but the service was always something of a Cinderella and it finally succumbed during a period of postwar financial stringency about two years ago.

This was not, though, the fate suffered by the long-distance Mersey–Tees–Tyne joint workings that through all the years of my association with them have seemed to possess a somewhat exotic air, but long though my memory is, it does not cover what must have been a very stirring period.

I have a series of bound trade magazines at home and in one of these there is a small paragraph which states that on August 3, 1927, a firm which is not named, but could have been the Leeds and Newcastle Omnibus Company, had begun to run four times daily from Newcastle to Leeds. The return fare was 15s (75p) and the journey took about $3\frac{1}{2}$ hours each way. Stops were made only at Gateshead, Chester-le-Street, Darlington, Northallerton and Ripon perhaps because of licensing difficulties.

It must have been a successful pioneering venture and so attracted competition, for by November 1927 the same journal was reporting that Messrs Bunting and Taylor had opened a route from Newcastle to Liverpool the previous month. The concern was running one bus each way per day, using vehicles of ADC or Thornycroft manufacture, and its arrival meant there were now *SIX* separate operators covering the roads involved.

Another innovation followed in October 1928 when the appropriately named Star Motor Services of Newcastle introduced an all-night service. This ran three times each way per week, on alternative nights, employed vehicles with 26 reclining seats, and issued rugs and pillows to every passenger, but it is to be hoped heaters featured as well, for Standedge can be a very chilly spot in midwinter.

Yet another would-be operator that same

As mentioned in the text, road surfaces around 1934 left a lot to be desired. Note the variations in the foreground plus the hazards presented by relaying. Car 107 was one of the last trams to be acquired by Halifax.

year was the Gladwyn Parlour Company of Manfield Woodhouse who in November were reported to be considering a Liverpool to Leeds route, but the fate of this and that of the other contenders is not reported so presumably they moved out as the bigger concerns moved in.

The first to appear was Northern General that began to operate daily from Newcastle to Liverpool in May 1928. This must have been a super express venture as there was no facility at all for the carriage of passengers between intermediate points, but that situation was partially rectified with effect from May 15, 1929, when the first joint limited stop service began. This linked Manchester or Leeds with Newcastle and was provided by the Northern General, West Yorkshire, Yorkshire WD and North Western concerns, when presumably the Liverpool service was withdrawn.

From July 1929 East Yorkshire joined the pool, and Manchester to Hull or Bridlington bookings could be made, but this facility did not survive for many years as East Yorkshire withdrew, thereafter maintaining a Leeds to Hull service that was run jointly with West Yorkshire, and of course continuing to run from Leeds to Bridlington.

Later in 1929 one pool trip per day was re-extended to Liverpool and from April 16, 1930, that seaport became the regular western terminus, but it was not until May 1931 that Lancashire United joined the pool when the hourly service—it worked jointly with North Western from Liverpool to Manchester—was included. The pool arrangements, incidentally, became most complicated as the northern operations of the Fawdon Bus Company, which had run between Newcastle, Leeds and Birmingham, were continued under the original name after take-over on March 1, 1933, in partnership with the existing joint facilities and then from October 18, 1933, the Newcastle to Liverpool via Bradford service of Tyne and Mersey Motor Services Ltd was included after purchase by the partners.

The future pattern was now largely set, but one big variation has still to be recorded for on August 1, 1933, United took over the Leeds and Newcastle Omnibus Company workings and appeared on the route which linked the two terminals named in the original owners title two days later. All the pool partners (except East Yorkshire) then made application to incorporate the former LNOC Middlesborough and Northallerton services into Liverpool to Leeds "short" workings together with the joint United/West Yorkshire Leeds to Middlesborough service which was then extended to Redcar during the summer (and so continued until the outbreak of the war) and had been in operation from August 31, 1932.

The Commissioners refused the application in February 1934, but the case was granted on appeal and so on October 21, 1934, United Auto joined the Liverpool to Newcastle pool as a full member.

After all this it was no wonder that I was impressed and so it was always with pleasurable excitement that I would take my seat in one of the luxurious and fast machines, invariably employed, that contrasted so strongly to the native Tilling-Stevens and hear my father ask for, say, return tickets to Leeds, Newcastle or Dewsbury, our destination depending upon which branch of the family was about to be favoured with a visit.

The conductor would then wedge himself up against a handy seat-back and begin to write out each ticket separately before issuing them from his Bellagraphic machine. The wedging, incidentally, was an essential part of the process, because by the time the scribbling began the driver would be working our conveyance up to around maximum speed and road surfaces in, say, 1934 were actually rather worse than they are today.

We had some very sprightly runs from time to time although it was a Yorkshire Woollen District Leyland that shattered all records—and our nerves—but nevertheless none were so fast as to prevent me taking in the Huddersfield transport scene and this was certainly the best period to indulge in such an occupation.

I soon discovered that the Corporation had some very venerable tramcars of singularly antique appearance possessing as they did, short upper saloons—which had very low windows, no canopies over the balconies, and in many instances a different colour, for the undertaking had embarked on a livery change involving a lighter shade of red instead of the original dark brown that would not have looked out of place in Oldham.

Unfortunately, the express buses did not pass through the centre of the town but made a small diversion to reach their stop in Venn Street which had some merit in that it took one right past the Longroyd Bridge tram shed, which then had bays at 90 degrees to the present layout, and invariably opened doors, the Karrier works and over a short stretch of the Newsome route in South Queen Street where there was a loop and often two cars passing, usually of the aforementioned old-time style.

After leaving Venn Street you could see the wiring of the first trolleybus route to Almondbury, opened on December 3, 1933, and often one of the six trial three-axle buses as well. Then our vehicle gained Leeds Road and with that important thoroughfare the remainder of the Marsden tramway route which ran out to Bradley, so one was able to gain a full picture of the scale of operations along this 10-mile-long double-tracked trunk route.

From about 1934 though these journeys across Huddersfield became all the more interesting as miles of trolleybus overhead wire were strung up, and then came various service changes, my old Marsden reverser going out of use on April 9, 1938. Another interesting point was the cutting back of the Bradley route to Deighton railway bridge so that the road under that structure could be lowered to allow free passage for the trolleybuses, which came into full use on June 10, 1938, a shuttle being provided by motor buses whilst the work was in progress.

The Huddersfield Joint Committee motor

A totally enclosed Huddersfield car stands on the Brighouse route with Bradley Woods and the reserved track section in the background.

bus fleet, like that in Halifax, had had a strong Karrier flavour, but similar policies were being followed with the steady elimination of these machines and their replacement by AECs, a process that could well have been facilitated by the readiness of the Southall concern to participate in part-exchange deals, but in Huddersfield the diesels took second place to the Corporation-owned trolleys which boasted an exotic red/brown/cream livery until about 1936 when the swirls that one associates with the streamline era of the late 1930s came into vogue.

Bradley terminus boasted another trolley reverser in tramway days and then one left the tram tracks before crossing the Calder Bridge and heading for Dewsbury.

A few yards after running under Cooper Bridge station came the Three Nuns Hotel and I well remember on my first ever trip being told that Robin Hood was alleged to be buried in the grounds of Kirklees Hall hard behind that holstery, but I received this piece of information with some scepticism for had not the gentleman roistered around Sherwood Forest close by a Nottingham that to my boyhood mind was almost as remote from the Three Nuns as the moon.

There was, though, a sort of ecclesiastical flavour apparent a few miles further along the road when a bend in the road revealed the Ravensthorpe terminus of the Yorkshire (Woollen District) Electric Tramways whose single-deckers ran out to the point from Dewsbury, their home town. These cars were noteworthy to the writer in carrying a large brass warning bell which hung under the canopy at the driver's end, and that individual gave notice of the approach of his steed by shaking the leather thong attached to the clapper, but then they were about as old as their route which dated from March 15, 1903.

The Dewsbury system and the even more remarkable one run by the Dewsbury & Ossett organisation were obviously on their last legs and were only encountered on about three occasions. The last Dewsbury tram ran on October 31, 1934 (actually number 11), when Leyland double-deckers took over, but they too possessed an unusual characteristic in that centre entrances became the order of the day.

At this time and until well into the postwar period all YWD vehicles were finished in a rich brown/cream colour scheme that was always maintained in a most immaculate condition and was so much more attractive than the inevitable red that came to be applied around 1950/1951—or the latest manifestation to white national poppy/white—but there were few thoughts in this now bygone age of large-scale rationalisation and even the Mirfield to Dewsbury length, despite being in the heart of YWD territory, boasted a couple of independents, namely Wood and Longstaffe whose vehicles still ply the route to this day.

I will leave further mention of the Dewsbury district until later and go on to the final section, thence to Leeds, which was always to my mind the least interesting part of the trip, although I was always intrigued by the poles obviously provided for electric traction purposes along the last mile or so of journey from the Whitehall Road cattle market into the City Centre but there was no trace of any attendant tramway track so I came to the conclusion, rightly as it turned out, that here was an early casualty, only what I did not know was that the trams had been withdrawn on June 15, 1922, eleven years after the initiation of the pioneer trolleybus service to Farnley, an event that took place on June 20, 1911, simultaneously with a similar event in Bradford so that one City could not be accused of stealing a march on its neighbour. I only wish now though that I had been able to see those trolleybuses and in particular the later Bishop front-wheel-drive machines that must have been quite something.

After crossing the river Aire our long-distance bus would turn off to the left under the low bridge that took the trains into Central Station in order to reach Wellington Street and the West Yorkshire bus station of that name where a halt of about 30 minutes would be made for longer distance passenger refreshment purposes—but there was one momentous occasion when our tyres trod a different path.

I cannot after this length of time remember whether we actually picked up a regular service vehicle which was scheduled to make the diversion or whether it was a special event but I suspect the former as this second route was certainly followed in the early postwar days.

On the particular occasion, however, I had no inkling that we were going to do other than travel via Dewsbury until, after leaving Venn Street, we kept straight ahead and began to follow tramcars carrying the destination Brighouse. In hardly any time at all the tracks swung left into a most unlikely-looking opening and vanished among a large clump of trees. Our bus, though, continued on the main road to Bradley Bar and then dropped down into Brighouse to meet the tramway tracks again just above the station bridge.

The cars terminated in the middle of the town a few hundred yards further on and here were both Halifax buses and the signs that yet another tram service had reached the same place, as indeed was the case until May 6, 1931, when the Halifax cars had been withdrawn, and petrol-engined AEC double-deckers provided in their place.

I did not realise at the time that Halifax trams had actually reversed in Brighouse until March 31, 1929, after arriving from Halifax (except at those times when either a local shuttle or the express tram service was operating) and before continuing along the Bradford road to Baliff Bridge. Through tramway connection from Huddersfield to Bradford was not of long duration because

Bradford is a much-changed city. About the only building still standing is the office of Woolcombers Ltd on the left, only now it houses the City Transport Department, an organisation long since bereft of its tramcar fleet.

the Huddersfield to Brighouse service was not opened until 1921, but for the few years when it was the sole alternative to rail the need to make two changes brought forth many complaints, and here was a ready-made opportunity that the private bus firms of Calder Bus and Hebble were quick to seize in the mid-1920s.

Hebble became established on the Bradford–Huddersfield bus route, which was now worked in full conjunction with those two municipalities, in January 1927 but Halifax buses were no longer to be seen in my day as they had departed from the Brighouse–Baliff Bridge section on December 31, 1929, and also off a local Halifax–Baliff Bridge service about the same time, despite the fact that this had run every 30 minutes. This rather uninspiring place did have some interest as YWD vehicles crossed the main road in their journeys from Leeds or Cleckheaton into Halifax involving negotiation of an almost incredible gradient in the process —but more important still tramway track and overhead came into view once more.

No tram was to be seen, and I was sure we should be meeting one en route for the terminus ere long but we seemed to go quite a way before we reached Wyke and such a vehicle, yet another of the blue Bradford balcony types.

The Baliff Bridge section was so long a-dying that the route must have almost created a British record for semi-survival as the final full day timetable was worked on November 8, 1932, and yet the trams to both Wyke and Bradford lasted until June 11, 1944. The final demise was brought about not so much due to desire but by the condition of another length of reserved track, this time in the mid road position, that ran from Low Moor almost to Odsal where we regained some familiar roads. In later years I was able to ride along this part of the Bradford system but to my everlasting regret I was unable to sample that missing Huddersfield line which I found later also used a reservation through Bradley Woods in order to gain Rastrick and the street-laid single track and loops that led thence to the Brighouse

Station, even though I often visited Huddersfield and saw the Brighouse trams running prior to June 30, 1940, when they too gave way to trolleybuses that used the main Bradford road to Bradley Bar, in preference to the woodland path.

Their stay in the area was, however, none too long as the Brighouse section was to become the first Huddersfield trolleybus casualty, being cut back to Bradley Bar on July 9, 1955, but I often felt in the immediate postwar era in view of the interest then being displayed by both municipalities in two wire traction that a through Huddersfield–Bradford trolleybus route was an almost certain possibility. In the event here was just another "might have been".

This chance journey though was not yet ended as we passed through another West Yorkshire bus station, this time in Bradford, and then continued along the tramway that I have touched upon before to Stanningley where one encountered not only the Leeds trams running out to Pudsey but also the remains of that unique piece of tapering track that once allowed Leeds and Bradford to have a through tramway service despite the difference of $8\frac{1}{2}$ in in the gauge of their respective tracks.

The Pudsey route continued in use until December 31, 1938, but Leeds cars were to come out to Cohens Foundry or Half Mile Lane for years to follow and closure did not take place until October 3, 1953, an event that saw the return to traffic of quite a number of buses that I had come to know in the final prewar years.

Unfortunately, my space allotment has now been used up and so I shall be unable to mention my trips into other parts of Yorkshire on this occasion, but perhaps if the Editor agrees I can continue with chapter 2 in a later *Annual*. Meantime, might I express my thanks to the general managers of the West Yorkshire Road Car Company, and the Corporations of Huddersfield, Halifax and Bradford for their assistance in providing the illustrations and a good deal of historical information.

Contrasts in the Austrian Alps

Continental wanderings with D. FEREDAY GLENN

With the wider horizons of Europe before us, a brief look at Transport in Austria might be timely, as the contrasts to be seen today are as exciting as any—and in very beautiful surroundings. The primary stepping-stone for any tour of Austria begins, naturally, at Innsbruck in the Tirol. Local services in and around this lovely city, surrounded by mountains, are provided by the IVB with trams ancient and modern, motor buses and a skeleton service of trolleys. In addition the State Railway (ÖBB) offers some feeder services connecting with the trains at the Hauptbahnhof using Saurer buses, including some normal-control models, in an attractive blue livery. Inevitably there are the yellow/black vehicles of the Postbus services; even here one may find an odd Saurer with the "vintage" look of a normal-control model. Finally one should not overlook the large number of excursions that visit Innsbruck bringing anything from a double-deck "Skyliner" coach manufactured in Stuttgart to an elderly Krauss-bodied normal-control Mercedes like the one I saw in May 1972 on hire to the ÖBB for their service to Telfs—an immaculate bus, at least 20 years old.

Other cities such as Salzburg, Graz and Vienna (Wien, capital city on the Danube) can offer trolleys (Salzburg) or trams (Graz or Wien) and assorted colours of local buses including three-axle double-deck Büssing examples in the capital. Most private railway systems also run buses, so you have the Stm.L.B. in Styria, GKB from Graz and the Zillertal in the Tirol—quite an eyeful!

A long way from home, former Hants & Dorset Bristol K6A 1111 with rebuilt Strachans utility body to the unique style of H & D descends from the Katschberg Pass through the narrow arch at Gmünd on an enthusiast's holiday tour of Austria in 1970.

Curious is the least extravagant
epithet used to describe the large,
Austrian-built Steyr seen here at
St Pölten in the familiar Postbus
livery.

Outside Innsbruck Hauptbahnhof,
IVB tram 8 with two ancient
four-wheel trailers awaits custom
for the next journey to Solbad Hall
(service 4), while a Gräf und Stift
(since withdrawn) collects
passengers on service F.

Veteran Gräf und Stift, built in Wien in 1951, still at work with the Steiermärkischen Landesbahn (Stm LB) in June 1971 at Weiz.

Henschel articulated trolleybus 33 pauses in the main street of Kapfenberg (Styria). Noteworthy is the extensive advertising and the unusual colour scheme of cream/grey.

Under the eye of the Castle, old and new Mercedes buses of the Stm LB pause for a lunch-break at Murau, Styria. The modern two-door bus is the first of this design to join the Stm LB fleet; the side destination indicator is another innovation.

The Stm LB operates buses as well as trains. Here at Murau are two of the smallest buses used in such rural areas: a Hanomag (*left*) and the small 1951/2 Steyr. Note the roof racks and the ski-rack fitted to the Steyr; livery is two shades of green.

Preservation Progress

KEITH A. JENKINSON describes the growth of the movement

London Transport's pioneering efforts in the preservation field are well known. The 1920 K type is seen en route to St Helens in 1969, where it was to join in a celebration parade.

Since its inception some seventeen years ago, many developments have taken place within the commercial vehicle preservation movement, some of which have been for the better, whilst others can be said to be questionable. In order that these developments can be reviewed, it is, of course, necessary to look back to 1956, the year when it all really began.

For a number of years people had been preserving and restoring old cars and traction engines, but until then no one had taken any positive action to save any old buses, lorries, vans or fire engines from possible extinction. Although some serious thought had been given to these larger vehicles, the only ones preserved at this time were a handful of early buses owned by their former operators and one or two commercials that were in the hands of private individuals. Thus, in 1956, when a small group of enthusiasts in London decided to buy an old bus, they were thought to be somewhat more than eccentric. The vehicle they chose was an AEC Regal single-decker dating from 1929 which had originally been operated by London General Omnibus Company, passing to the newly formed London Transport in 1933 as their fleet number T31. This was a very interesting vehicle, the last survivor of its type, and had lingered on long after all its contemporaries had been withdrawn and sold. It was with this bus that the commercial vehicle preservation movement can be said to have been born.

After completing the purchase of this venerable machine, the next step was to restore it to its original condition, but here things did not go as smoothly as planned. Due to undercover accommodation being unavailable in which to house this bus, work had to be carried out in the open, at first on a public car park, and this made restoration extremely difficult. To add to this problem, it was found that the bodywork was in a far worse condition than had been originally thought, but then, this is a story of its own, too lengthy to relate in this restricted space. Suffice to say that the foundation had been laid for what was to become in future years an increasingly popular activity.

On hearing of this venture, it was not long before other bus and commercial vehicle enthusiasts were spurred into action, having seen that preserving these large relics was not so much a pipe dream as had been previously thought. Very soon the number of buses saved from the breakers' torch had reached double figures, and was increasing almost month by month.

One of the most popular sources for these old buses was Jersey, where many of those still in daily service dated from the late 1920s or early 1930s. These were, of course, all in good condition, which meant that they could be restored with reasonable ease, and in 1958 no fewer than twelve of these buses had been shipped back to the mainland to join the growing collection that was being built up. With one exception, all these ex-Jersey buses were Leylands, albeit of different types, consisting of long and short wheelbase Lions, TD1, TD2, Cub, Cheetah and a couple of beautiful Lioness models. The odd man out was a Dennis Ace with a somewhat unusual full-fronted body.

By this time, clubs were being formed to cater for this new interest, and it was not long before the Vintage Passenger Vehicle Society, Historic Commercial Vehicle Club and London Vintage Taxi Club could all boast of growing membership with additional vehicles. Amongst these new acquisitions were a number of interesting buses, some of which were of once-familiar makes that were, alas, no longer to be seen on our highways and byways, such as Reo, Chevrolet, and Gilford, a Morris Dictator, a Thornycroft and a Maxwell, all makes which had almost been forgotten despite their popularity in prewar days. However, after all these wonderful old vehicles had been saved and restored to their former glory, the next question was what to do with them. It seemed pointless somehow to carry out all this work if they were then to be hidden away for only their owners to admire. Surely they should be shown to everyone, for the basic aim of the preservation clubs was to restore these vehicles in full working order, but how, and where? With this thought in mind, it was decided to hold a rally, similar to those enjoyed by the old car and traction engine enthusiasts, where all these old commercials and buses could be displayed for everyone to see. And so, in 1958 the first true vintage commercial event was held, thc venue being Leyland Motors factory in Lancashire. This was a great success, so much so that it was decided to hold another rally later in the year, this time at the works of the rival manufacturers, AEC Ltd, at Southall. In comparison with present-day events, both of these were very small, but at least a start had been made, and their success set the pattern for the future.

The next few years saw a continued steady development in all directions with more and more vehicles being bought for preservation, and rallies spreading further afield. As far as buses were concerned all those being preserved were of prewar manufacture, and by far the largest proportion were single-deckers, possibly due to the fact that they were easier to accommodate, and did not require the amount of work needed to restore their larger counterparts. Leyland products continued to hold the lead in numbers, although by now most other makes were at lcast represented, and together they were building a comprehensive history of road passenger transport.

JUB 29, a 1928 Leyland Titan TD1 with 1932 Eastern Counties body, is a well-known rally entrant. It is seen at Battersea at the start of the 1970 Brighton run.

A major step forward came in April 1962 when the three clubs merged into one, taking the name of the Historic Commercial Vehicle Club. This enabled all those interested in old commercials, whether buses, lorries or fire engines, to work together for a common cause, and in doing so, strengthen even more a pastime that was increasing in popularity.

The first event to be organised in the name of this new enlarged Club was one which has now become a legend, known throughout the world. This was, of course, the London to Brighton Run which was inaugurated in May 1962, and looking back it is difficult to imagine that this Run, which is now supported by over 200 entries, started off with less than 40. Such is the progress that has been made within the preservation movement in such a short span of time. However, returning to 1962, it is true to say that despite the fact that the HCVC was supposedly a "national" club, up to this time almost all the buses and other commercial vehicles which had been preserved were domiciled in the south of England. Apart from a few exceptions, this interest did not begin to spread to the midlands and north for another couple of years or so, and consequently the majority of the events organised for these larger vehicles tended to be concentrated in the southern counties.

By 1964, the scene geographically was beginning to change, and the absorbing interest of commercial vehicle preservation was starting to creep into the provinces much more quickly than it had done before. More buses were being added to those already restored, filling many of the historical gaps that still existed, and double-deckers were becoming more fashionable as collectors

A 1937 Bristol JO5G with ECW body, showing the results of one night of vandalism, following over a year of hard restoration work.

pieces, to be seen at almost every rally. Despite the fact that bus preservation was still to a large extent in its infancy, the general standard of restoration was good with almost everyone who owned a vehicle taking a tremendous pride in it, and doing his best to rebuild it as near to its original specification as possible. How times have changed since those days. . . .

The next few years saw a continued spread of this pastime to almost every part of Britain, and to stimulate this, a number of additional rallies were introduced, with those at Ipswich, Liphook, Woodcote, and Rugeley developing into annual events, whilst gatherings at Stamford Hall and Bramcote were of a less regular nature. At all of these it was encouraging to see the number of preserved buses growing, and to find new acquisitions mingling with those which were already becoming well known, creating an air of excitement wherever these vehicles were to be seen.

Towards the end of the 1960s, the bubble suddenly burst, and it seemed as if everyone now wanted to jump on the bandwagon. This caused a rapid increase in the number of buses being purchased for preservation, followed by a dramatic growth in the number of rallies organised to cater for all these extra vehicles. Added to all this was the postwar bus, which began to make its appearance in no small way. Hitherto, postwar buses had been generally regarded as being too modern to evoke any real interest, and indeed even today many still hold this view. It was, however, inevitable that sooner or later buses of this period would start to be preserved, for if not, then they too in the future would become just as difficult to find

A 1936 Commer N4, JG 7763, with rare 26-seat coach body by Reall, photographed on a London-Brighton run.

as their prewar ancestors were already becoming. Thus the advent of these postwar examples at first seemed very necessary if a total history of transport was to be maintained, but as their numbers increased, one began to question the wisdom of this. Whereas with the prewar buses there was very little duplication of types amongst the preserved, it was the complete opposite as far as the postwar vehicles were concerned. Many of these were identical vehicles, differing from each other only in livery, this being borne out by the numerous Bedford OBs, Leyland PD2s and London RTs, to name but a few, which can be seen at rallies throughout the country. Whilst it is true to say that everyone has a perfect right to preserve the vehicle of his choice, it in a way seems somewhat wasteful to save so many identical vehicles when there are still a number of types which as yet are not represented at all. With many of these newer buses came a new breed of preservationist— if preservationist is the correct term to use. These can be best described as the "Instant Motorists", whose main reason for buying a bus appears to be so that they can play at "Bus Drivers". Restoration to them seems to be very much a secondary consideration, as can be seen when their vehicles appear at rallies, and ultimately many of these buses will no doubt return to the scrap yards from whence they were acquired, to be lost for ever. I hasten to add that fortunately not all the postwar buses preserved are owned by this type of person—indeed many are restored to a very high standard, and are a credit to their owners.

Turning again to the rally scene, it now appeared as if everyone wanted to cash in on this extremely popular activity, and the motoring calendar had never before been so full. Several events were scheduled practically every weekend in different parts of the country and it was totally impossible for anyone to attend them all. Some were well organised specialist events catering solely for commercial vehicles whilst others were merely added attractions for local carnivals or galas. The road run type of event was becoming

extremely popular, and in addition to the annual London to Brighton Run a number of others were being promoted, themselves to become annual fixtures in future years. Amongst these were the Hull to Scarborough Run, the Rochdale Motorcade, the Robin Hood Run, a picturesque run along the Scottish coast from Dunbar, and the Trans-Pennine Run from Manchester to Harrogate. This last-mentioned event across the bleak but beautiful Pennines is now regarded as one of Britain's premier rallies, attracting over 150 vintage commercials each year, a large proportion of which are buses. There are also the static events, where all these magnificent vehicles of years gone by can be seen, some of which are those held each year at Ipswich, Godalming, Weymouth, East-bourne and Hamilton, and, of course, there is the Bus of Yesteryear Rally—the largest all-bus rally in Britain—which at first was held at Stratford-on-Avon, and has now been moved to London. Whilst on the subject of rallies, it would be remiss of me not to mention the working museums, where old passenger vehicles can be seen and travelled on. There are basically three of these at present: the tramway museum at Crich, the trolleybus museum at Sandtofts, and the East Anglian Transport Museum at Carlton Colville, where buses, trams and trolleybuses can all be seen working side by side, capturing many memories of past decades.

Moving on to the 1970s, it is pleasing to find that hitherto unrepresented makes of vehicles are now being added to the ever-growing list of the preserved. BMMO buses have at last begun to appear, as an example of operators own products, and Sentinel have joined the ranks of the now obsolete makes. A Guy Wulfrunian, never seen in large numbers other than with West Riding, is now in an advanced stage of restoration whilst memories of the famous East York-shire domed roof buses specially built to pass under Beverley Bar live on with a few preserved examples of this now extinct breed. Two more road rallies have been added to the list, these being the Birmingham

EA 4181, the preserved 1929 Dennis E which was
West Bromwich 32, refuels at Todmorden on the
1970 Trans-Pennine run.

Above: A fine example of an early passenger vehicle, a 1913 Model T Ford with 14-seat country bus type body, leaving Brighton.

The Dunbar rally has attracted an increasing number of passenger vehicles each year. These four vehicles at the 1972 rally are an ex-Alexanders (Northern) Leyland PS1/Roe, an ex-Alexanders (Fife) Guy Arab III/Craven, an ex-Red & White Guy Arab III/Duple and the Eastern Scottish all-Leyland TD5 open-topper.

Outer Circle Run and one from Bournemouth to Bath, further emphasising the continued growth of the preservation movement.

So much for the past and present, but what about the future—what new developments will the next 17 years bring? This, of course, is anyones guess, and without the aid of a crystal ball, one can only surmise.

Looking back over the 12 years that I have been actively connected with the preservation movement, it is sad to think of all the buses which could have been saved, but were not. These are now lost for ever and in most cases cannot be replaced. As every year rolls by, prewar buses become more difficult to find—although some do still exist. These are generally in very poor condition, requiring an enormous amount of hard work to restore them to their former glory, but as has been shown in the past, this is by no means impossible. Obviously the future will see at least a few of these veterans saved, whilst at the same time, for a variety of reasons, the scrap yards will no doubt claim some of the vehicles at present preserved. Buses which are today familiar sights in regular daily service will be replaced by new models, and will disappear completely unless some are acquired for ultimate posterity, and one cannot help wondering just how long it will be before a Leopard, Atlantean, Fleetline or Routemaster will join this elite band, or the hundredth Bedford OB, Leyland PD2 or London RT is preserved!

The limits and restrictions imposed by the authorities upon the number of vehicles allowed to participate in any one rally will no doubt force the organisers of these to be more selective, resulting in only the older or better-restored vehicles being accepted and repetition being eliminated, and whilst in many ways this will be unfortunate, this stage is already being reached at the premier events. More stringent MoT tests and new legislation will compel a higher standard of restoration and may possibly cause vehicles to be altered from complete authenticity to comply with these, unless exemptions are granted. All this will make preservation

Last-minute attention to GWT 630, an ex-South Yorkshire 1947 Albion Valkyrie CX13 with Burlingham body.

more difficult, but whatever the future has in store, of one thing I am certain. This is that commercial vehicle preservation is here to stay, and will continue to grow from strength to strength, resulting in a complete living history of road transport which future generations will be able to see and admire.

Little did those pioneers know in 1956 that what they were doing was to snowball into something which would sweep the country in such a short space of time, and it is to them that we should be so grateful.

Suffolk Independence

Photographs by G. R. MILLS

Above: Chambers, Bures HWO 339, an ex-Red & White Guy Arab III/Duple, at Sudbury in 1969.

An older Chambers' Guy, Roe-bodied Arab II GV 9614 at West Bergholt in 1963.

Amos, Belchamp St Paul JVX 307, a 1944 Bedford OWB/Duple, shortly before withdrawal in 1964, at Ovington.

Foot of page: Mulley, Ixworth BGV 155, a Bedford OB/Mulliner, at Sudbury in 1962.

Right: Norfolk, Nayland CCF 574, a 1950 Austin CXB with Mann Egerton 31-seat body, at Boxted Cross in 1968.

Above: Norfolk, Nayland FOF 296, an ex-Birmingham all-Leyland TD6c, at Stoke-by-Nayland in 1962.

Right: A more recent Norfolk double-decker, BDJ 70, an ex-St Helens AEC Regent RT type with Park Royal body, seen in 1966.

Osborne, Tollesbury 29, KXW 356,
an ex-London Transport all-Leyland
Titan RTW type, at Layer in 1967.

Theobald, Long Melford, BDR 269,
an ex-Plymouth Leyland Titan TD5
with a 1953 Leyland lowbridge body,
at Long Melford in 1964.

Goldsmith's unusual CCF 777, a Vulcan 6PF of
1950, with Dutfield 29-seat body, seen at
Sicklesmere in 1961.

Squirrell, Hitcham MUN 91, a Bedford SBG/Duple,
passes an Eastern Counties Bristol SC at
Somersham in 1966.

The Postwar Explosion

JOHN PARKE on developments in the South-East

A Duple (Midland)-bodied
Leyland Tiger Cub on
Southdown service 19 at Lewes
bus station.

Whether or not the endeavours which are being made to check the gradual decline in bus traffic meet with success, it is probable that, so far as the British Isles are concerned, the late 1940s and early 1950s will come to be looked upon as the time when the road passenger transport industry was at its peak. Many circumstances favoured the operator. The end of World War 2 had brought a fairly rapid demobilisation of members of the Forces with their gratuities, more members of a family were often working so that the money available had increased and, pending the changeover of a substantial part of industry to peacetime production, many things were in short supply. Rationing continued in force for food and motor fuel and this too had repercussions on the bus industry. It was not easy to buy cars and, if they were obtained, there were obvious limits to the amount to which they could be used. Deliveries of goods by retailers were somewhat rare and the arrival of their supplies could be irregular. It followed that more frequent visits to the shops were often felt to be well-advised. In turn the demand for bus

services grew not merely for shopping but also for evening entertainment as it was going to take some years for television to become universally available.

There had, of course, been changes in bus services during the war with new services introduced where it was felt to be justifiable. More noticeable, however, had been the tendency to use larger buses with double-deckers replacing single-deckers and with bigger single-deckers replacing smaller ones. The fact that regional transport commissioners had been willing to consider one-man operation of normal control buses seating more than 20 passengers had been another important factor and had influenced the 32-seat capacity of the Bedford OWB. Such developments were to prove of some help as was possession of any of the buses produced to wartime specifications. It was nonetheless clear that many operators were going to need to work very hard to meet traffic demands. Many of their vehicles were elderly and it had not been easy to keep them fit bodily and mechanically. The likelihood of rapid delivery of new ones was small

DRB 793, a Leyland Cub of Ashline, Tonbridge, reverses at Sevenoaks Weald.

An Ashline ex-Southdown Dennis G at Hildenborough en route to Tonbridge from Underriver.

and, at the outset, those available would be needed to supplement rather than replace existing fleets.

There had during the war been a certain amount of replacing single-deck by double-deck bodies on suitably shortened chassis and this process was to continue in the post-war years, even in some cases with postwar chassis where the pattern of operating needs had changed. More frequent, however, was the rebodying of old chassis or fairly substantial reconstruction of existing bodies. Relaxation of wartime austerity requirements took some time and, apart from all else, there was an obvious need to replace the wooden slatted seating with something a little more comfortable. It was true that the travelling public was prepared to endure quite a lot in gratitude for transport being there at all, but there were limits, particularly if the journey was of some length. Seats from withdrawn buses were used when available, but they were not all that plentiful and sometimes tended to take up more space so that a reduction in seating capacity resulted.

Despite vehicle problems, and in the earlier stages something of a staff shortage, operators were prepared to meet public demand to the best of their ability. Initially wartime licensing controls were retained. The area traffic commissioners had been replaced by a regional transport commissioner, who was generally the former chairman of the commissioners, and he had very considerable powers. Public sittings had been suspended for the most part, although there had been a few instances where objections or representations had led to special sittings. There were to be some more of these before the gradual reversion in 1946 to the old licensing procedure. Some operators were better placed than others to provide new facilities and in certain cases those who felt themselves to be at a disadvantage protested vigorously if they considered that the proposed operations would abstract traffic from existing services or from those which they planned themselves as soon as they were in a position to provide them. When they did occur such hearings tended to remind one of the early days of licensing when sounds of competitive strife

An ex-Plymouth Dennis Lance of Hants & Sussex at Graffham, with another in the background.

A Hants & Sussex Bedford OB in Emsworth on the service to Rowlands Castle, begun in 1948 and withdrawn 2½ years later.

echoed through the traffic courts.

The use of bigger buses which was mentioned earlier had been made possible on some routes by authorising them on hitherto restricted roads so that, to cite but one example, STL type double-deckers on London Transport's country service 421 from Sevenoaks to Heverham via Otford and Kemsing were sailing on every journey past a notice which restricted the road to buses carrying not more than 15 including the driver. There were many other examples and quite soon after the war there was a certain amount of trouble with councils and, very occasionally, the police who wanted a reversion to the former conditions. This it might be added brushed aside such matters as the absence of suitable vehicles, the loads being carried, and so forth. The commissioners were nearly always unmoved, but looking back now it is possible to see here one of the early examples of the unsympathetic attitude of non-bus-owning local authorities towards operators.

Fuel allowances had been eased from early in 1945, although the restriction on Sunday morning operation remained for another year—it had been introduced in January 1943—and one of the first undertakings to initiate new routes was Southdown Motor Services Ltd. There were comparable moves in other parts of Britain, but since the editor requested something about southern England these notes will be concerned mainly with events in Kent, Surrey and Sussex, to put those counties scrupulously in alphabetical order. Southdown had always been an enterprising operator and it came as no surprise that its plans were well advanced. It should perhaps be added that in the west and north-west of its territory its hand had been rather forced by ambitious proposals put forward by Hants & Sussex Motor Services Ltd and its associate companies. Independent operators of stage services had long been relatively few in south-east England so that it came as something of a surprise that H & S, Beacon (L. B. Atkins), of Crowborough, and Sargent's Service, of East Grinstead, should be among the more energetic proponents of expansionist policies. Another independent had, as a matter of

A Southdown rear-entrance Leyland Royal Tiger in its first days of service in East Grinstead on route 36.

fact, made an even earlier move. This was Ashline Ltd, of Tonbridge, with an old-established service thence to Underriver. For most of the war it had been operated on Saturdays only, but late in 1943 a proposal was put forward for weekday operation and for the introduction of another weekday service from Tonbridge to Sevenoaks Weald via Hildenborough and Southwood. The Underriver service also worked through Hildenborough but with a protective fare and a restriction on local traffic to safeguard London Transport. The new proposals envisaged the carriage of local traffic and the LPTB was decidedly pained especially as it too linked Tonbridge and Weald, albeit by a different route. Ashline was only seeking three journeys on each route on Mondays to Fridays and six on one and seven on the other on Saturdays. The LT headway on the common section was mostly quarter-hourly and its opposition failed.

Relatively soon after the Ashline success there had been moves for new services in West Sussex and in the summer of 1944 the South Eastern Regional Transport Com-missioner held two public hearings. They resulted from rival applications by independent and large operators. Mr B. S. Williams proposed a Wisborough Green–Haslemere service via Kirdford, Plaistow and Gospel Green which would connect at the last-named with his service to Midhurst. That route had been started on November 30, 1943, as a revival of a Midhurst–Lurgashall licence held by I. A. Gavin but not, in fact, used. Mr Williams, who had taken over the Gavin business, sought also a permit for a service from Kirdford to Slindon via Petworth, Sutton, Bignor and Bury which would connect with Southdown services at Petworth and at Slindon with the Silver Queen service to Bognor Regis. Aldershot & District objected to the proposals and countered with others for the extension of its Godalming–Dunsfold service to Petworth via Plaistow and Kirdford and for two new routes from Haslemere to Lurgashall via Gospel Green and to Horsham via Gospel Green, Plaistow and Loxwood. In the upshot the Williams permits were refused and the only A & D success was the extension of the Dunsfold

A Maidstone & District Leyland Tiger at Stangrove Road, Edenbridge in 1951.

A Maidstone & District Dennis Ace at Tonbridge on the ex-Ashline service just after it was taken over in 1948.

service. Some reference was made to the existing service from Plaistow to Horsham via Loxwood which was operated by F. H. Kilner, and this was perhaps prophetic for the battle over this area was to break out again when the Kilner business came into the B. S. Williams sphere.

Mr Williams was also concerned in the other hearing with a proposal for a service on three days a week from Chichester to East Marden via Chilgrove. The Southdown counter-proposal was for a two-days-a-week service between Chichester and Petersfield via Chilgrove, North Marden and South Harting and succeeded subject to consultation between the Commissioner and his opposite number for the Southern Region— the old division had reappeared as a wartime measure. This was not, however, the end of the large operator's problem. W. A. Potter, who had services from Midhurst to Bepton, to Stedham and to Petersfield via Linch and Hillbrow, proposed a Tuesday and Thursday service from Midhurst to Elsted via Didling and Treyford. Elsted had been unserved since Southdown had, under instructions,

cut back its Petersfield–Elsted service to East Harting at the beginning of the war. It now sought to restore the full route and to extend it via Elsted Station to Midhurst. Its application was granted and it must be said that Mr Potter really had no chance. The roads he sought to use were bad and the facilities could not compare.

These decisions did not end rivalry in West Sussex. The Wallings wished to dispose of the old-established service running as Silver Queen between Slindon and Bognor Regis and Mr Williams formed a subsidiary company to take it over. He had also plans for integrating it with his own operations but Southdown objected and opposed an application for transfer of the licence to the new company. The objection succeeded and the service was sold to Southdown in February 1945. That company was also introducing other facilities as opportunities arose and permits were forthcoming. The Chichester–East Dean service was extended via Goodwood to Chichester, making it a circular route, and town services were instituted in Lewes. In March 1945 B. S. Williams was authorised

Left: A Maidstone & District Leyland Tiger at the Friars Gate terminus of the route from Edenbridge to which Sargents' had extended the service in July 1949.

Right: London Transport Leyland Cub C19 at Oxted Station on the first week of operation of route 494.

to extend the ex-Gavin Midhurst–Graffham service to Petworth and in the same month there was something of a wrangle further north when Aldershot & District and Yellow Bus Service applied jointly for a new local service to the Rydes Hill Estate in the north-west part of Guildford. Two other operators, Crouch and Safeguard, were anxious about the effect on their existing services and when the joint application was granted Safeguard was given a service to Northway just south of the estate and Crouch received some extra journeys.

Guildford was not the only area to see developments—in fact the unpreparedness of some of the roads in the estate delayed implementation of the grant in full. South-down introduced 35 from Petersfield to Fareham via Clanfield and 35A from Peters-field to Chalton and Maidstone & District, which, with wartime traffic demands in the Medway towns, was somewhat hard pressed for both staff and vehicles, indulged in one or two moves such as extending its Faversham–Lenham service to Grafty Green over a piece of road long unserved by

anyone.

More was to come and this time it was the most substantial Southdown change so far. Pressure on its well-established service 30 from Brighton to Chelwood Common (con-nections with East Grinstead) which runs by way of Hassocks, Burgess Hill, Haywards Heath, Lindfield and Horsted Keynes had been building up steadily and extra capacity had had to be provided on the Brighton–Haywards Heath section—it may be recalled that vehicles used on the main service included the four Leyland Tiger six-wheelers from the peacetime Eastbourne–Beachy Head route. From May 13, 1945, two new routes were introduced—32 and 36—which ran two-hourly and combined with 30 to provide a half-hourly service between Brighton and Horsted Keynes. The 36 had a slight inter-mediate difference in that it ran via Keymer between Hassocks and Burgess Hill instead of via Friar's Oak. At Horsted Keynes the 36 turned north to Sharpthorne, whence it double ran to West Hoathly, Tyes Cross, Sainthill Green and East Grinstead. These points were already served by the 87 service

ex-East Grinstead Coaches (Sargent) but the Horsted Keynes–Sharpthorne and Tyes Cross–Sainthill sections were new. The 32 stayed with the 30 to Danehill and then turned south to Sheffield Arms, Fletching, Piltdown, Maresfield and Uckfield. Save for odd garage journeys the road from Danehill to Piltdown was unserved, although, until its withdrawal in November 1939 Southdown 28 had covered the Danehill–Sheffield Arms section. This was the East Grinstead–Lewes–Brighton service bought from East Grinstead Coaches in 1933. A year later the route of 32 was varied further to run via Buckham Hill Turning between Piltdown and Ringles Cross, thereby covering more roads for the first time.

Southdown was certainly getting under way and in July 1945 it restored its Little-hampton–Storrington service, linked it with the Storrington–Thakeham service, the route number of which—71—it took because its old number had gone to the ex-Silver Queen service, and extended the route to Coolham over the 75. Maidstone & District then took steps to reduce pressure on its service 5 on the section between Hurst Green and Hastings. It cut back its Tunbridge Wells–Sandhurst service (80) to Flimwell and projected every third journey to Hastings via Hurst Green and Battle—the Flimwell–Hurst Green road was new. The Flimwell–Hawkhurst–Sandhurst section was covered by extending the 84 (Tonbridge–Tunbridge Wells–Flimwell). Two years later the service was to be extended further to Bodiam and Hastings.

The year had been quite a good one and so were those that followed. So much was this the case that it is necessary to confine mention to a few. London Transport was short of vehicles but it did manage to introduce the 494 between East Grinstead and Oxted via Crowhurst early in 1948 covering many new roads and employing for a period one of the CRs, while in the summer of that year it introduced a section of 424 between Horley and Outwood Common and a year later a further variant between Horley and Horne. Further west a more daring effort began in March 1950 with 449 from Dorking to Ewhurst via Capel, Ockley and Forest

Green. It is a great pity that it did not endure. Beacon, of Crowborough, to which brief reference has already been made, increased days of operation of its service to Uckfield via High Hurstwood from two to three early in 1946 and introduced also a town service in Crowborough, while Sargent's of East Grinstead stepped its service thence to Edenbridge up to daily. Two years later came a major reorganisation with a new Edenbridge – Cowden Crossroads – Crowborough service connecting with a Cowden Crossroads–East Grinstead service and also an East Grinstead–Larches–Ashurstwood route. These passed to Southdown in March 1951 and in September of that year to M & D. Both those companies had been developing in the interval. In the spring of 1946 the latter commenced 107 between Tunbridge Wells and Chiddingstone covering between Saints Hill and Chiddingstone new territory to all intents and purposes, although there had been a West Kent Motor Services route through Chiddingstone Hoath in 1928–29.

In June 1946 Southdown opened more new ground by extending its 86 (Haywards Heath–Balcombe) to Turners Hill and initiated 98 from Seaford to Golden Cross via Alfriston, Berwick, Chalvington and Ripe. As usual with this company it managed to achieve a remarkable number of connections. Shorter M & D extensions were the spur off 24 from Yalding to Laddingford and taking 53 beyond Mereworth to West Peckham, while a new 110 from Mayfield to Tunbridge Wells via Wadhurst covered mostly new ground between Mayfield and Wadhurst. In the summer of 1948 came the extension of 22 from Crowborough to Brighton as 122 and its joint operation with Southdown as a through Gravesend–Brighton route. So the process continued and it is one of the things that has to be regretted that so much of this enterprise received indifferent reward. It is equally to the credit of the earlier managements that they should have judged correctly with the earlier developments and that it should generally have been those which have survived the recent economy measures.

Left: For a period after its start, London Transport 494 was worked by a CR type Leyland Cub.

Sargent, East Grinstead Bedford OB in Edenbridge with an ex-Southdown Tilling-Stevens of Ashline behind.

Second Hand

Acquisitions by larger companies, photographed by GAVIN BOOTH

Rochdale bought the former demonstration Daimler Fleetline KKV 700G, seen here as Selnec 6038 in 1971.

Chester Corporation acquired this 1951 AEC Regal III/East Lancs from Nottingham. LTV 700 is seen in Chester in 1967.

City of Oxford 205, a 1961 Weymann-bodied Leyland Atlantean acquired in 1970 from South Wales.

Red & White U65.51, a Lydney-bodied Leyland Royal Tiger acquired from United Welsh, seen in Pontypridd in 1963.

Some Glimpses of Buses on the Isle of Man

Examined by A. MOYES

One of three 1964 Leyland PD3A/1s in the Isle of Man Road Services fleet, 68 (68 UMN) squeezes through the narrow streets of Castletown, September 1972. It originally bore registration 8 MAN, but was re-registered in 1970.

Isle of Man Road Services Dennis Falcon/Strachan
29—ex-Aldershot & District—on the quayside at Peel
in July 1970, backed by fishing boats.

The Isle of Man has traditionally had much to offer to the transport enthusiast. The well-known splendours of its century-old steam narrow-gauge railway (now sadly attenuated), the magnificent trams of the Manx Electric Railway, and the Douglas Corporation horse trams are all, to a greater or lesser extent, publicised tourist attractions in their own right. As with most islands of its size (30 miles long and 10 miles wide), it has the advantage of being not too large to be confusing, and yet to have sufficient variety to justify yet another repeat visit. As far as buses are concerned, many facets of vehicles and routes have been well-documented, largely due to the work of W. T. Lambden, a former Omnibus Society Chairman and now general manager of Isle of Man Road Services. For strict vehicular details, readers are referred to various publications available from the main enthusiasts' societies. Yet one sometimes feels that transport enthusiasts who visit the Island are so seduced by the obvious charms of Victorian railed transport that they neglect the attractions of the buses and their routes.

NOTE: *At the time of writing, negotiations were proceeding between Douglas Corporation Transport and Isle of Man Road Services with a view to the latter absorbing the municipality's transport operations. This article thus concentrates on facets of operations on the Island which are least likely to be altered by any merger, and on pure nostalgia. It is hoped that it will at least provide a context against which a possibly interesting post-merger phase in 1973/4 may be placed. Much of the article refers to conditions applying in 1972.)*

All-Leyland Royal Tiger of IOMRS, 89, at Baldwin on
an evening run from Douglas in May 1970.

It would be logical to begin at Douglas, the
Island's largest town, chief resort and
destination for the Isle of Man Steam Packet
Company's sailings from Liverpool, Belfast,
Dublin, Ardrossan, Fleetwood, Heysham and
Llandudno. On leaving the sea terminal
buildings, one is likely to be confronted with
Douglas Corporation's buses on the forecourt,
decked in a Bournemouth-style maroon-
banded yellow livery. Like most operators
on the Island, the Corporation's fleet is
geared to sharp summer peaks, when the
Island's resident population of 56,000 is
swollen by a summer total of almost half-a-
million visitors. For this reason alone, old
vehicles used to enjoy long life on the Island,
working feverishly in the few summer months,
and being lovingly cared for during the long,

quiet winter. Thus until the late 1960s the
stud awaiting the more popular sailings at the
sea terminal would have included surely the
last full utility wartime Daimlers in the UK,
and a fine 1939 AEC Regent II with a
Northern Counties body of a design introduced in 1933—now preserved in England,
though disguised with a Yorkshire registration.
Park Royal-bodied Leyland Comet single-
deckers and GS-like Guy Vixens would have
been another mouth-watering *hors d'œuvres*
for the unprepared. Unfortunately for the
enthusiast, the need for increasing one-man
operation to cut costs brought about the
purchase of eight Leyland Tiger Cubs with
Duple Donington bodywork from Lancashire
United for the 1970 season, sweeping away
the Vixens, the utilities, and the two unique

The last of the batch of five Mulliner-bodied Guy
Otters which Douglas Corporation ran from 1957
to 1970, 12 (WMN 488), enters town from Port
Soderick in 1967.

Regent RTs with Northern Counties body-work.

What remains in the Corporation's fleet is certainly not without interest, however. Indeed, because there is little market for scrap on the Island, and shipping costs to the mainland are so high, many of its withdrawn vehicles can be found in varying stages of disintegration in farmyards over the Island and even capable of operation, in corners of depots. The active Corporation fleet contains a high proportion of sonorous AEC Regent IIIs dating from 1947–1949 and handfuls of later Regent Vs, bodied by MCW (some with vast indicator blinds) and Willowbrook. The Regent IIIs seem to find favour on the year-round operations. These are more or less restricted to two suburban routes ending in inter- and early postwar corporation housing estates—Pulrose, to the west of town, slightly off the main road to Peel, and Willaston, which sits quite loftily on Douglas's north-west edge. A third, shorter in-town service to Ballabrooie often keeps one of the small 1967 Bedford single deckers occupied—if not very well-loaded—most of the day. A circular route employing older AEC Reliances and Regal IVs virtually completes winter operations. In summer, ephemeral routes appear like mayflies, giving this town with its resident population of 20,000 a dispro-portionately dense route coverage. The principal addition is a frequent service (appropriately numbered route 1) along the almost two-mile long sweep of promenade, serving many of the larger hotels, the beach, and the Manx Electric Railway's terminus at the northern end of the bay. It also competes almost inch-for-inch with the Corporation's seasonally-running horse trams, which usually make a profit, whereas its buses do not. Seasonal routes also take its buses outside the town boundaries south to Port Soderick, both by an inland route also served by Isle of Man Road Services, and a coastal one along the Marine Drive, which until 1939 boasted an electric tram service.

Visible from the exit to the sea terminal is Lord Street bus station, which is the focus for Road Services operations as well as acting as terminus and standing ground for several Corporation routes. The splash of red livery may well have swamped the Corporation's yellow by the time this is read, though some Isle of Man Road Services (IOMRS) dual-purpose single-deckers are in a predominantly grey livery. Technically, it is still associated with the Isle of Man Railway, and its original role was indeed to reinforce the Railway's hold on the Island's trunk routes outside Douglas. Under the General Managership of Mr A. M. Sheard, it evolved a *modus operandi* which remained unchanged for many years. To generalise, key routes fanned out from Douglas to all the towns on the Island—northwards to Ramsey, west to Peel, and south-westwards to Castletown, Port Erin and Port St Mary. Each of these ran at similar frequency and for many years were the preserve of the 22 all-Leyland PD2/1s and PD2/3s which entered the fleet from 1949 to 1951, though on the flatter Peel route the eleven shorter-winded 1946/1947 PD1s shared. The PD2s also dominated the frequent suburban Douglas–Onchan circular. From the more important sub-depots, less frequent cross-country and local routes filled in the network. Peel and Port Erin depots shared the route linking them over the hills via Castletown, and Peel and Ramsey depots similarly shared the linking route via Kirk Michael. Ramsey depot catered for routes looping over different parts of the Island's hummocky northern plain, amongst others. On all of the lesser routes, a vehicle pattern had emerged in the early 1950s which was to

last until Mr. Sheard's retirement in 1966. Utility Bedford OWBs were regular performers on Peel's local trips except for rosters to Castletown, which invariably featured one of the quartet of ECW-bodied Leyland PS1s. Another of these would appear on the Ramsey-Andreas-Bride circular service, and PD1s, misleadingly labelled "Airport", worked the circular to the former RAF base at Jurby. Two rather complicated routes from Douglas into otherwise empty quadrants (north-north-west to Baldwin and due west to Foxdale), both the preserve of Leyland HR40 Olympics, completed virtually the whole network in the 1950s and early 1960s. Seasonal variations in the timetables were relatively modest, many summer excess needs being met by duplication—and by the high carrying capacity of the Isle of Man Railway. Allocations of vehicles to routes were, as mentioned, almost unchanged from year to year, with the proviso that later Orion-bodied PD2s and PD3s gravitated to the Douglas–Port Erin and Onchan circular routes.

The years of Mr Lambden's occupancy of the IOMRS general managership have seen radical changes away from long-established route patterns and introduced more variety and unexpectedness in the rostering of, and variety of, vehicles. Firstly, one-man operation had previously been limited to a few workings by OWBs (the later trio of OB buses hardly ever appeared other than on schools workings). Yet the existing fleet contained several buses immediately convertible to omo—the eight Olympics, the seven dual-purpose Tiger Cubs, and four solid all-Leyland Royal Tigers. One of the Royal Tigers had run less than 4,000 miles per year in Sheard's day, mainly on contract runs to Ronaldsway Airport from Douglas. Beginning in January 1967, all of these were converted to omo. In April of that year, the faithful ECW-bodied PS1s were withdrawn, along with all of the OWBs and OBs. These smaller vehicles were replaced by seven of the Strachan-bodied Dennis Falcons then being withdrawn by Aldershot & District. From the same source came enough Setright ticket machines (in-

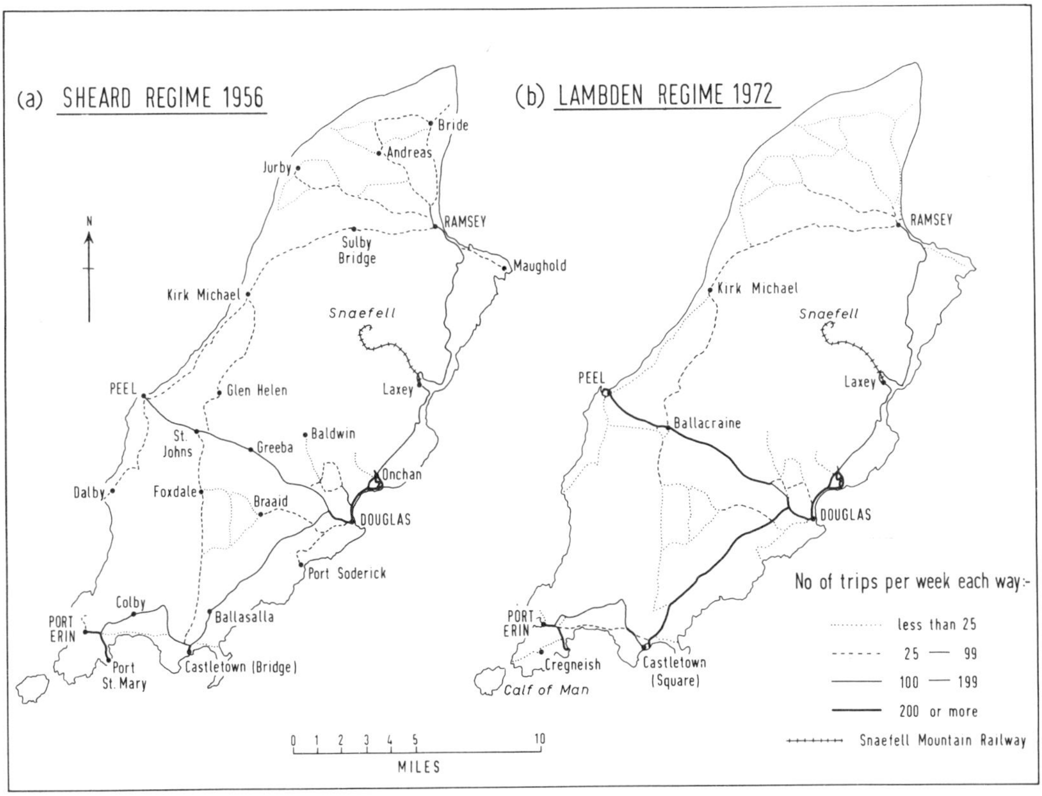

A comparison of summer peak frequencies in the periods of managership by the previous and present general managers of Isle of Man Road Services.

The last surviving Bedford OB on the Isle of Man is MMN 215 of Highlander Coaches, seen here picking up excursion passengers at a tram and bus stop on Douglas Promenade.

itially used as insert models) to sweep away the slower Bellgraphic system. By 1972 coaches and dual-purpose vehicles, hitherto rigidly kept away from stage work, were providing omo stage duplicates. In addition, nine Leyland PD3s, originally with Stratford Blue but arriving via Midland Red, were purchased early in that year. The intention was to extend omo into the realms of double-deck operation on the trunk services with their moderate winter loadings—indeed heavy loadings during the school terms. Secondary education is to some extent concentrated in Douglas and this generates substantial school traffic. For 1973, after the arrival of six more Stratford Blue PD3s, it was expected that only four all-Leyland PD2s would remain in service.

Each year since 1966 has seen some innovations in the company's timetables, which have been accompanied by a more flexible attitude to vehicle rostering. On summer Saturdays in 1972, consecutive turns on the Douglas–Peel route were provided by a Dennis Falcon, an ex-Stratford Blue PD3, an all-Leyland Royal Tiger, duplicated Leyland Olympics and finally an all-Leyland PD2. Numerous route alterations have been made which generally represent tidier or more commercially minded variants on the established route pattern; some of these will be mentioned in considering some possible trips around the Island by bus. As the maps show, the route alterations have strengthened the main routes radiating from Douglas at the height of the season. Douglas is, after all, the base in which most bus-using holidaymakers are likely to stay; the limited-stop timings which have been introduced on the Port St Mary, Peel and Ramsey routes are testimony to the rather weaker intermediate trip demands. The Peel–Ramsey and Peel–Castletown services have been pruned to a varying extent, the former almost to extinction, but its reasonably populated northern end has been covered by extending the Douglas–Ballacraine–Kirk Michael service northwards to Ramsey. To some extent this replaces the sadly closed Douglas–St Johns–Ramsey railway line.

Let us imagine two circular trips from Douglas which give an idea of the use which might be made of Road Services' "anywhere" tickets (lasting one day or one week) at the peak of the season; the precise timings might not be operating in 1973 or 1974 but the gist is clear.

A productive first day could involve leaving Douglas at 9.50 am on the limited-stop run to Port Erin, which will probably produce an ex-Stratford Blue PD3. This whirls fairly swiftly over the undulating green countryside, with occasional glimpses of the sea, as far as Ballasalla. Here, the surviving line of the Isle of Man Railway, with its equipment dating from the 1870s, is crossed on the level, and then, ironically, within half a mile on the left appears Ronaldsway, the Island's civil airport, well-appointed to deal with the traffic of the 1970s. Soon one is approaching Castletown, originally the Island's capital. Thanks to the strengthening of the bridge across the harbour, it is possible for our PD3 to swing across this once-restricted structure and worm its way through the narrow main street to pull round into the square, dominated by the limestone walls of Castle Rushen. Then follows a fast run along the southern plain to Port Erin along the Shore Road. At Port Erin Railway Station there would be a good connection onto an Olympic for a sortie to the southern tip of the Island, via the thatched village of Cregneish. At the terminus at the Sound, a narrow strip of threshing water separates the "mainland" from the Calf of Man, an islet to which boats sail from Port St Mary. Returning to Port Erin, its marine biological station could be visited, and an ECW-bodied PS1 noted acting as a crew room at the IOMRS depot, before having lunch.

One could then return to Castletown by the more inland, original route serving Colby and Ballabeg, and at the Square pick up the 2.30 pm Peel bus. This takes one over the hills to Foxdale, where the lead-mining booms of the nineteenth century have left a fascinating series of monuments. To the east of Foxdale, the sparsely populated country is served by a somewhat thinned tangle of a service linking St Marks, Eairy and Braaid

Isle of Man Road Services ex-Stratford Blue and Midland Red Leyland PD3/Northern Counties 57 running alongside the harbour at Peel on the service from Douglas.

Low cloud shrouds the summit of the Calf of Man, seen behind IOMRS Leyland HR40 Olympic 50, at the Sound, July 1972.

with Douglas. When the TT races close the main road from Douglas to Ballacraine, the main Douglas–Peel service runs over these by-roads, but is thus restricted to single-deck operation by the low railway bridge of the Foxdale branch which survives at Lower Foxdale, though unused for more than 30 years. Now travelling down-valley, one soon reaches St Johns, where the Island's parliament is annually promulgated, and makes for the sea at Peel. This town, still renowned for its kipper-curing factories, is well worth an inspection—the cathedral on St Patrick's Isle, the old huddled streets, and the harbourside, along which most buses from Douglas run on a one-way circuit of the town before plunging into its heart to find the bus depot. A there-and-back trip could be fitted in to Dalby on a timing which, in winter, would be likely to produce a Falcon. The main road back to Douglas follows the low-lying corridor formed by the valleys of the rivers Neb and Dhoo. After St Johns, points of intermediate interest include the romantic shell of Greeba Church, occasional glimpses of the abandoned railway line to Peel, and—probably nearer to a busman's heart—a contractor's yard on the outskirts of Douglas containing two former Douglas Corporation Leyland Comets. On arrival in Douglas there would be time to sample the 5.15 pm to Baldwin before having a meal. A pleasant run this, but the best way to do it would be in winter on the school bus—for road reasons this has to be a Falcon—which serves both the beautiful West and East Baldwin valleys.

A second day's circuit could start on the 9.45 am to Ramsey via Kirk Michael. After serving some suburbs of Douglas rather circuitously, this strikes the main road to Peel once again. At Ballacraine, however, we turn right, following the TT course through lovely Glen Helen, then pursue a fairly level but slightly winding course at the base of the hills which fill much of the northern half of the Island. At Sulby Bridge, one can recall the Manx Electric Railway's one-time seasonal service thence almost to the summit of Snaefell to connect with its Snaefell Mountain section. Ramsey is noteworthy for being the

The only horse tram still bearing the legend "Douglas Corporation Tramways" as opposed to "Transport" is enclosed car 18, which is generally used only in inclement weather.

northern terminus of the Manx Electric Railway's line up the east coast from Douglas; the station is a short walk from the IOMRS depot/bus station, but the sight of one of the 1893 tramcars more than justifies the effort. Probably most would feel that it offers a much more characterful way to return to Douglas than the direct IOMRS bus. Before making the journey southwards, however, one could make a circuit of part of the northern plains, preferably on the run round Andreas and Bride, rather than the duller Jurby circuit.

After this, the reserved tracks of the Manx Electric Railway must surely draw one southwards, snaking round the headlands, along the cliff tops and circuiting deep wooded glens to Laxey. Here, the Snaefell Mountain Railway, with its 1895 electric cars, begins its coggy journey to the summit of the Island's highest peak—Snaefell's 2,034 ft. Laxey is situated in a cleft with the famous wheel (the "Lady Isabella") which used to pump the once-prolific lead mines dry, some way above the small town, and the MER station. The beach is almost a mile downhill in the other

One of two Bristol RELL6Ls with Duple Commander IV bodywork delivered to IOMRS for the 1970 season. 38 (38 UMN) seen here at Rushen Abbey on a South Midland tour in July 1970. All IOMRS coaches except for this pair were transferred to the tours (IOM) company in 1972.

direction, so reasonable business is done by A. R. Caine, who runs Ford Transits between the Wheel and the Beach in the season—the only other stage carriage operation on the Island apart from IOMRS and DCT. The Manx Electric Railway then provides an exhilarating run back to Douglas, hiding itself behind the houses of South Cape, weaving from side to side of the main road, assuring its right-of-way by tram-activated traffic-lights, and, if the visibility is excellent, affording a sight of the outline of the Lake District fells 50 miles away across the Irish Sea. It is appropriate that one of IOMRS's progenitors was promoted by Cumberland Motor Services. These nostalgic thoughts are probably forgotten by the time that the Douglas terminus at Derby Castle is reached. Here, both the MER car sheds and the Corporation's horse tram depot are situated. An appropriate way to end the day's jaunt would be lulled by the rubber-reinforced hooves of a 14-hand horse and the rhythmical thump of the rail joints.

It would be incomplete to leave the Island without some brief mention of coach opera-tion. However, operators have been radically thinned in numbers, and vehicle variety sadly reduced in comparison with the palmy early postwar years. In 1972, IOMRS, which had been accumulating coach work since 1966 and had bought an interest in Corkills and Hamills, the largest coach firms in Douglas, welded these into Tours (IOM) Ltd, which uses the fleetname "Man-Intourist" (from this one conjures up visions of burly Russian tourists thronging the "round the island" tours). The other operators are now much enamoured of Bedford SBs. By the 1972 season, only one Bedford/Duple OB was active on the Island, and it will be a sad day when Highlander Coaches put this last survivor of a type once so familiar on the Island, away for winter for the last time. One can find consolation in the glimpses of buses, coaches and trams on the numerous old postcards still available on the Island. These, and vintage MER Edmundson geographical tickets are good souvenirs to take back to the mainland—to remind one of the need to pay another visit to the Isle of Man.

Prewar Postscript

Photographs by G. H. F. ATKINS

A smart **TSM** with Weymann body, operated by Notts & Derby, in Nottingham, April 1933.

An ex-Peterborough Electric Traction Co SOS taken over by Eastern Counties at Leicester Southgate Street, August 1935.

One of ten AEC Regents with Hall Lewis bodies operated by Nottingham City Transport, February 1935.

Foot of page: One of the small fleet of Duttons "Unity" Services, later taken over by Trent. It was a Dennis Lancet with Willowbrook body, August 1935.

An unusual purchase by Yorkshire Traction was this batch of six Daimler CP6s with Brush coach bodies, seen in Nottingham, August 1934.

Foot of page: A London Midland & Yorkshire services Leyland Tiger with Beadle body on the London-Bradford run at Nottingham in March 1934.

A Harrogate Carriage Co Tilling-Stevens coach on a holiday cruise in July 1928, seeking guidance in Weston-super-Mare.

Foot of page: A vintage London General selection in Whitehall in June 1932.

A London-Newcastle coach of Majestic Saloon
Service in Grantham High Street in June 1931. It
was an AEC Regal with Duple body, and behind
is a De Dion Bouton of Wilks Parlour Car Services
on the Leeds-London service.

Foot of page: One of a batch of Leyland Tigers
with special coach bodies, also by Leyland, used
by Western SMT on the London-Glasgow service,
in Grantham, August 1935.

West Country Matters

Photographs by R. L. WILSON

Southern National 1779, a Bristol LS5G with ECW body at Weymouth in 1959.

Devon General 830, an AEC Reliance/Weymann near Morchard Bishop in 1971.

Western National 881, a Bristol K6A with lowbridge
ECW body, at Dartmouth in 1963.

Wilts and Dorset 273, a Bristol K with lowbridge
ECW body, at Salisbury in 1959.

Gloucester G1153, a Bristol **RELL** with **ECW** bus body, in Gloucester in 1970.

Bristol 7082, a Bristol **FLF** with **ECW** body, in Gloucester bus station in 1970.

Bath Services 2979, a Bristol MW with ECW body, in Bath in 1971.

Cheltenham District 79, an Albion CX13 with ECW body, in Cheltenham in 1959.

Covered Wagons

IAIN MacGREGOR *illustrates two colourful examples*

Overall painted buses advertising Barclaycard have appeared in several cities. This is Glasgow LA230, a Leyland Atlantean/ Alexander, on Glasgow Bridge in March 1972.

An earlier overall painted bus, photographed by R. F. Mack in 1955. Leeds Corporation AEC Regent/Roe 263 (GUA 788), decorated to publicise a National Savings campaign, at Bramley.

London Transport started the recent craze for advertising buses. RM249(VLT 249), publicising Unipart, is seen at Earls Court.

I was a Teenage Bus-spotter

GAVIN BOOTH wallows in nostalgia

The first shock came when my grandfather broke it to me that tram conductors did not keep the money they collected. My initial reaction was of complete stunned disillusionment—my second was to reshape my future, and tram conducting was relegated to join professional footballing and engine driving in the ranks of abandoned careers. Yes, engine driving, for I passed on to buses via railways, but after several locospotting summers underlining Gresley Pacifics in my *ABC of British Railways Locomotives* I exhausted all the engines that seemed likely to work into Edinburgh and then moved on via trams to buses.

Thus, in 1955, a 12-year-old locospotter became a 12-year-old tram and bus spotter, and that wasn't quite so easy. It was natural to assume that I was a lone pioneer, as there were no *ABC*s covering Scottish buses, and there did not appear to be any organisations catering for my particular interests. There were, of course, as I eventually discovered, but in many ways this sense of exploration was more exciting. I compiled my own fleet lists, which make amusing, though surprisingly accurate, reading now. The natural assumptions were the problem. I happily attributed Edinburgh Corporation with more buses than they really had by assuming that they always bought in nice round numbers, and always filled gaps in the numbering system; similarly, because Leyland announced in bold letters that they had built the bodies on a batch of Edinburgh Titans, I innocently assumed that AEC had built the bodies on some AEC Regent IIIs. Needless to say they hadn't, and gradually the real picture began to form—but I sometimes feel that we have become very sophisticated today, with fleet lists and the like generally available and with the weekly and monthly trade papers pouring out masses of advance information, which seems to preclude many of the genuinely exciting "discoveries" I can recall from earlier days.

Most schoolboys usually have an intelligent interest in the forms of transport they regularly use, and in 1950s Edinburgh this meant trams. From a fairly early age I

deducted that there were four main types of tramcar in service, flat-topped cars, domed-roof cars, streamlined cars and "the Manchesters" — obviously there were subtle variations, but this proved to be a relatively accurate breakdown. We conveniently moved house shortly before our local tram route was about to succumb to the all-conquering bus, to another part of the city where the trams were destined to rattle past our door for another three years. And rattle they did, for the trams on route 21 were "the Manchesters"—11 ex-Manchester Pilcher cars which were restricted to this service because of track clearance problems. Everyone knew "the Manchesters"—even though they weren't too different from the Edinburgh domed-roof standards—as they were fast, powerful cars, and the track to Levenhall was none too good in places. My parents certainly knew them, and if there was a choice of trams at the Post Office terminus, safety would come first and

Not AEC bodies as I had naively assumed, but Brockhouse bodies were fitted to Edinburgh's small batch of AEC Regent IIIs. 232 in Princes Street in 1960.

they would elect to ride on a standard Edinburgh car.

Gradually the buses took over, and I still kick myself that I fell asleep before the last 21 tram passed my bedroom window on November 13, 1954. The replacement buses were Metro-Cammell-bodied Leyland Titan PD2/20s, from orders that eventually totalled 300, and they looked very modern with their tin fronts and simple interior finish, a contrast to earlier deliveries. Previously my main contact with Edinburgh Corporation buses had been on regular visits to grandparents who lived on routes which boasted suitably interesting buses. One, the 29, was operated by buses from the 1952 batch of 21 all-Leyland PD2/12s, solid, attractive and popular buses. The other, the 15, was the haunt of four Crossley SD42/6s with front entrance Roe bodies, intended for Waldie of Helensburgh but diverted to Edinburgh in 1948. Crossley chassis and Roe bodies were rare

enough in Scotland, but in many ways the main novelty was the door position—the Edinburgh single-deck fleet was otherwise composed of rear entrance vehicles, including 16 1952 Royal Tigers. The Crossleys were never really happy, and were unused between 1954 and 1957, when they were withdrawn and actually sold for further service, rare for Edinburgh buses at that time.

The mid-1950s, when I first really got to grips with the Edinburgh fleet, was a particularly interesting period. Most fleets were at this time. As a result of World War 2 there were elderly time-expired buses, unfrozen and utility buses, rebodied and rebuilt vehicles all over the country. Edinburgh had been a Daimler stronghold in the 1930s, but the War had introduced fresh faces, and by 1955 there were also AECs, Bedfords, Bristols, Crossleys, Guys and Leylands, and the Leylands were rapidly dominating the fleet. The oldest Daimlers really dated back to

Another Brockhouse body, this time on one of 15 Bristol L6Bs in the Edinburgh fleet, with a Guy/Metro-Cammell following, at Clermiston in 1959.

1932, but had been rebuilt and rebodied. The oldest unrebuilt Daimler single-deckers were 1938 COG5s, the oldest double-deckers 1936 COG6s. There was a fair intake of Bedford, Daimler and Guy utilities and a varied selection of postwar buses, including a batch of 72 Birmingham-style Metro-Cammell-bodied Daimlers which worked the bulk of the longer-established bus services while the newer Leylands, together with rebodied Edinburgh Daimlers and London Guys, worked the tram replacement services.

The Scottish Omnibuses fleet in 1955 was, if anything, more interesting. Many prewar vehicles, rebodied and unrebodied, were still in service, AEC Regals and Leyland Tigers and Titans, and there were Guy utilities and postwar AECs, Bedfords and even, since SMT sold out to the BTC, Bristols. Like Edinburgh, SOL had a batch of rebuilt ex-London Transport Guys, but these had become single-deckers, and were rarely seen in Edinburgh as they were allocated to depots in the Borders. There was another oddity, S1, the SOL-built predecessor of the Albion Nimbus, which was also intended for Border routes, and when it was operational that's where it would be. But it was not really successful, and ended its service days ig-nominiously, running between Bathgate and Bangour Hospital. S1 was withdrawn in 1962 and became a mobile fish and chip shop in Dalkeith.

That was the Edinburgh picture in 1955, with added variety offered by the "independent" Stark, running apparent "SMT" buses on the joint Dunbar–Edinburgh route, and Wilson of Carnwath operating a variety of vehicles on the irregular Forth–Edinburgh service. Company operators running on joint services with SOL were Ribble, with Tigers, Royal Tigers and Tiger Cubs, United, with Bristol Ls and LSs and the occasional Leyland Tiger, and Alexanders, usually with Tigers, but also with newer AECs and Ley-lands. There was more than enough here to keep me busy. Everything was new and I hadn't tumbled to the fact that I could probably have got fleet lists from the operators I was "discovering".

Eighteen years do not seem a particularly long time, yet 1937 seemed an eternity away when I started, and I suppose 1955 seems equally distant now, especially when you consider just what has happened in the inter-vening years. Perhaps the most obvious change is the disappearance from our streets of trams and trolleybuses—still familiar enough sights in 1955. When the Edinburgh trams disappeared in November 1956 I had the foresight to apply for a place on the final procession. The last night was a spectacular farewell to a popular system, and an estimated 100,000 people turned out to pay their respects. After the excitement of the last night it was difficult to grasp that there would be no more of these rather stately four-wheelers grinding round our streets. Glasgow still kept its trams, of course, for another six years, and I spent many Saturdays on tram tours and last-day trips. The Glasgow "caurs" seemed to suit the city. Large, friendly, gaudy—the big Glasgow bogie cars were so different to their staid Edinburgh contemporaries, and yet they seemed very much at home among the Glasgow tenements. In the days before I was old enough to make these trips alone, Glasgow *en famille* always meant trams, the Subway and the escalators in Lewis's Argyle Street store—the only installation in Scotland at the time. In 1973 these attractions still prove a draw for my own son, although escalators are more common now and the only trams are to be found in the Museum of Transport.

I really started looking further afield in 1957, when a *Buses Illustrated* report that the two Leyland PDR1 prototypes had been sold to Lowland Motorways sent me rushing through to Glasgow. I had discovered *BI* in January 1956, and wasted no time buying up all the back numbers—though thankfully at this time this only amounted to 24 issues. I recently found a notebook containing details of that Lowland trip, filled with hastily-scrawled bus numbers—I was still suffering from the after-effects of locospotting and tended to note every bus I saw. In Glasgow that day there were a lot of buses about. I did find the PDR1s—both off the road—and lots of other fascinating Lowland vehicles. This was my first encounter with Lowland, and my last as it turned out, for at that time Lowland had only a few more independent months to run, and SOL took them over on December 30, 1957.

I had then—and maybe still have—an irritating tendency to find and photograph the *newest* buses in preference to the oldest ones. Admittedly the new buses of 1957 are rapidly becoming the old buses of 1973, but I can recall trailing my long-suffering parents down to Surrey Docks in search of London Transport RM1 in 1957; constant journeys to Hamilton to ride on the first Laurie Atlantean in 1960, only the second in Scotland; and even in 1972 travelling down to Newcastle to sample Northern General's first Leyland National—though it will be some time before these photos become historic.

The 1957 family holiday also took in East Anglia, and here were such delights as Eastern Counties rebodied Leyland TD2s and Great Yarmouth 1937 TD5s and wooden-seated utility Guys. It was also my first taste of the airy delights of open-top buses, with Great Yarmouth's 1934 AEC Regent/English Electric number 39.

In many ways, though, the most significant personal event of 1957 was a visit to Scottish Omnibuses premises in Edinburgh with the Scottish Study Group of the Omnibus Society. Here I discovered that there *were* other enthusiasts, and at last I gained access to SOL depots where previously "No Admittance" notices had kept me at bay, being a coward at heart. Equally significantly, SOL unexpectedly treated us to a huge meal in the North British Hotel, and I still insist that it is pure coincidence that I joined the Omnibus Society almost immediately, and started work for SOL four years later.

1957 was a busy year in Edinburgh, and the Corporation was in the middle of all kinds of fascinating experiments. There were demonstrators—AEC Bridgemaster 9JML. Beadle Commer Chatham XKT784, Albion

A Scottish Omnibuses Bristol LS6G with 38-seat ECW body, on the Edinburgh City Sightseeing Tour at the Palace of Holyroodhouse in 1958.

Aberdonian TGB752 and Daimler CVG6 SDU711—and two highly unusual Edinburgh vehicles at the Scottish Motor Show in November. 822 was an Albion Aberdonian lightweight (4.12.3) with Alexander 43-seat bus body, which only lasted a short time before conversion for coach work, and 998, a Leyland Titan PD3/2 with Alexander 72-seat body, one of the first forward entrance double-deckers to the recently permitted 30 ft length. Then there were 10 unpainted Metro-Cammell-bodied Leyland PD2/20s, the last of the 300 tram-replacement vehicles, which lasted in this form until 1959.

The main SOL event was the opening of Edinburgh's bus station in April 1957, and vehicles from all Scottish Bus Group companies were exhibited there for two days before it became fully operational. It was left to SOL to spring the biggest vehicle surprise, one of 20 Leyland PD2/20s with Park Royal bodies ordered in a hurry when Glasgow abandoned their Airdrie trams. These buses were the only postwar Leyland double-deckers to be bought new when the Lodekka was the standard double-decker, and they were doubly interesting as they were mounted on chassis intended for Edinburgh Corporation.

Right at the end of 1957 SOL bought Lowland Motorways, and an assorted fleet of 36 vehicles passed into their hands. There was a mixed bag of AEC and Leyland single-deckers, and an even more mixed selection of double-deckers, including an ex-Glasgow Corporation Albion CX19, ex-Plymouth Leyland TD4s and TD5s, ex-Western SMT TD4s and TD5s, three TD5s with newer ECW bodies, ex-Western SMT utility Daimler CWA6s and 6 ex-London Transport Craven RTs. If that weren't enough, two of the rebodied TD5s had Beverley Bar roofs. Only the RTs and the ECW TD5s lasted any time, but there were also three newer Leyland double-deckers which lasted rather longer, two all-Leyland lowbridge PD2/12s and a PD1-engined PD2/20. It will be no surprise that the two prototype Leyland PDR1s were

Above: Crossley Bridgemaster demonstrator 9 JML at Sighthill terminus, Edinburgh, in 1957. The schoolboy with long trousers is the author!

Right: The result of our 1957 vigil at Surrey Docks, London Transport RM1 on route 260.

not involved in the deal.

From all of this it will be seen that this was a particularly interesting time, and a colourful one with the rash of demonstrators and the constant succession of repainted Lowland vehicles emerging from Marine Gardens. These tended to work in Edinburgh for a short time before returning to Airdrie, where they were based, and as a proportion of them were highbridge vehicles in an otherwise lowbridge fleet, they had to be used carefully. This care had even to extend to the main SOL depot at New Street, Edinburgh, where access is by an awkward low height ramp. Highbridge buses had to use the exit doors.

Our 1958 holiday introduced me to Ayr, and particularly to AA Motor Services, the co-operative independent that had—and still has—an interesting fleet. In 1958 it included ex-Glasgow and London Guy utilities, an ex-Young, Paisley, Leyland TD7, Guy utilities rebodied with Roe centre-entrance bodies—and so on. The seemingly endless stream of fascinating AA buses kept me riveted to the spot at the Boswell Park bus station in Ayr—unwisely, it transpired, for my one trip north to Ardrossan on GAG970, the massive-looking Daimler CD650, revealed all kinds of tasty morsels, hitherto undiscovered, like the ex-Edinburgh unfrozen Bristol K5G, trudging round Irvine on a local service.

Another 1958 holiday—in the loosest sense of the word—took me across to Ballykinlar in Northern Ireland for the annual school cadet force camp. Little chance here to see buses, except the UTA Tigers that took us across the border to Dundalk for our one day out, and the delightfully antique Violet Bus Service ex-DUT Dennis Lancet and Leyland Tiger that awaited me there.

Slightly nearer home, it seems amazing now what vintage gems could be found in regular operation in Scotland. In 1960, for instance, Alexanders still had some 500 prewar and wartime vehicles in its 1,900-strong fleet, and I only had to go to Falkirk

One of Edinburgh's unpainted Leyland PD2/20s with Metro-Cammell Orion bodies, at Clermiston in 1959. Now, with its brothers, repainted.

Sold for scrap by Scottish Omnibuses, BDR 255, an ex-Lowland/ex-Plymouth Leyland TD5 with Weymann body, in 1960.

to wallow in delightful Leyland Cheetahs, Lions, Tigers and Titans, all in immaculate condition, the oldest dating back to 1934. A 1958 trip to Millburn Motors, the Glasgow dealers, to see the two ex-Lowland PDR1s, for sale and awaiting buyers, revealed a yard full of ex-Alexanders, Central SMT and Western SMT Leyland double-deckers, some with original bodies, others rebodied during the War. There were also Western SMT utility Daimlers and Guys, Alexanders Cheetahs—in fact, many vehicles that today would cause any preservationist to froth at the mouth.

Meanwhile, back in Edinburgh, more demonstrators were going through their paces. There was AEC Bridgemaster 76MME, Bedford SB8 UNM606, AEC Reliance PNR891 and Daimler CVG6.30 VKV99. After all that, the next Edinburgh Corporation double-deckers to materialise, early in 1959, were five more forward-entrance Leyland PD3s, including one, 999, in a startling all-scarlet livery. There were new single-deckers too, the first sizeable delivery since 1952. After the experiments with the Beadle Commer, the Aberdonian, the SB8 and the Reliance, they materialised as 50 Weymann-bodied Leyland Tiger Cubs, in many ways the single-deck equivalent of the predominant double-deck type. Their arrival prompted the withdrawal of the last of the Daimler COG5s, some parts of which dated back to 1932, and a further 50 Cubs in 1960/1961 cleared the way for the last of the post-war rear-entrance single-deckers, Bristols, Daimlers and Guys, to disappear.

As it turned out, 1959 was a very colourful year for Edinburgh. As well as 999 there was Guy 959 in a cherry red livery, Leyland PD2/12 256 in a drab all-madder scheme with only a white band for relief, and the blue Walsall Corporation Dennis Loline 600DDH which paid a visit in April in exchange for an Edinburgh Leyland PD3. This experiment, and the trial colours, had little bearing on future deliveries and liveries —except perhaps to reaffirm Edinburgh's

AA, Ayr's magnificent Daimler CD650 with Northern Counties body, at Ayr in 1958, and now, sadly, scrapped.

Another fine specimen, an Alexanders Guy Arab with Roe body in the maroon-painted Kirkcaldy town service fleet, at Kirkcaldy in 1960.

view that madder/white Leylands were what was wanted.

Scottish Omnibuses managed to withdraw the last of its own prewar Leyland double-deckers and Guy utilities that year—though the Lowland take-over had endowed the fleet with more prewar Leylands and two utility Daimlers, and some of these were still in service in 1959. In fact the three rebodied TD5s lasted until 1962.

My parents had a happy knack of going on holiday to places packed with transport interest, and I was only too happy to go with them. In 1959 we visited Leamington Spa—not a great transport centre in itself, but a useful base for visits to places like Stratford and Coventry. In Leamington itself, though, there were attractions like Midland Red FEDDs and a six-wheel Leyland Tiger—ex-City I think—running for a local contractor. Stratford Blue provided immaculately turned-out Leyland Tigers and Titans, and Coventry Corporation, not surprisingly, Daimlers galore, with AECs, Guys and Maudslays thrown in for good measure.

So to 1960, the last year covered by this article. School holidays and my improving financial status enabled me to wander further afield, and I managed to cover most of central Scotland during the year. The added discovery of Kodak Tri-X film extended my photographic season, and my 1960 notebook contains details of these trips. Like a visit to Kirkcaldy in April to see the tremendous collection of old buses, used as showmen's vehicles, visiting the town in connection with the famous Kirkcaldy Fair, when the whole sea-front Esplanade was littered with delightful specimens, usually traceable to Scottish Bus Group fleets.

I spent a happy four days with a British Railways runabout ticket at the end of August, giving me the freedom to explore various centres with the minimum of expense and the maximum of free time. Centres like Falkirk, still thick with prewar Leylands; Hamilton and Airdrie, with the obligatory visits to Laurie and Baxters; Kirkcaldy, again with old Leylands and many, many utility Guys; and Ayr, with many of my 1958 AA discoveries still about, joined by the customary selection of new and second-hand goodies.

That same notebook reminds me that football matches were a rich source of visiting buses, particularly when the Edinburgh teams, Hibs and Hearts, played at home to Glasgow giants Rangers and Celtic. 120 buses brought Celtic supporters to Edinburgh for a Hibs match in October 1960, including Alexanders Leyland Cheetahs, and several other prewar Leylands. The biggest prewar Leyland discovery that year was LJ2941, a 1930 ex-Hants & Dorset all-Leyland Titan TD1 51-seater, still working for a Johnstone contractor, albeit with a Gardner 5LW engine, and soon bought for preservation. Unhappily, LJ found its way to the breakers, but a happier 1960 event was the eleventh hour rescue of WG1448, a 1932 Albion Valkyrie with Alexander body, which was the first positive step to preserve a Scottish psv.

At a time when buses more than 20 years old are comparatively rare in Scotland, the vintage variety of the 1950s leaves a vivid memory—hence my preoccupation with the older buses that we took so much for granted at the time. The end of the decade really marked the end of the road for old and rebodied vehicles; gradually fleets became more up to date, and while Alexanders still had over 300 prewar and wartime vehicles when the vast empire was split into three companies in 1961, by the early 1960s most operators had flushed out their oldest buses.

It's a cliche, I know, but 1960 was very much the end of an era for the bus industry. For me, on the verge of leaving school and starting a career, it was very much the start of one. My interest in buses was to face several tests—temptations like girls and beer, for instance—but seems to have survived, one wife and two children later, with perhaps, a different emphasis and a lazier approach.

On reflection, I was probably right to listen to my grandfather. There would have been no future in tram conducting after all.

Leeds Observed

Photographs by R. F MACK

Facing page, upper: Leyland Tiger TS8/Roe 20, at Oakwood carrying children and parents participating in a children's day competition. *Lower:* Daimler CVD6/Brush 529 in Woodhouse Street.

Above: AEC Regent/Roe 174 at Kirkstall Abbey.

Top: All-Leyland PD2 375 in Osmondthorpe Lane, passing under the Leeds-York railway line.

Above: Daimler CVD6/Roe 517 at Roundhay Park with Horsfield tram 203.

Top: **AEC Regent 111/Weymann 653 at Harehills.**

Above: **Daimler CVG6 544 in Woodhouse Lane,** passing a gang resurfacing after tram abandonment.

London Transport and Standardisation

JOHN ALDRIDGE examines the London approach

The London RT, the ultimate in standardisation. RT2659 in Trafalgar Square in 1972.

Standardisation is a great talking-point in the bus world today. We have the Five Cities bus in Holland, the German VöV standard bus, and the Leyland National in Britain and elsewhere.

But in volume these are probably all outpaced by standard designs adopted by London Transport and even the pre-1933 London General Omnibus Company. Of course, there is standardisation and standardisation. The German VoV bus standards are rigid: the dimension of almost everything is laid down —yet we hear that so far Mercedes (just one of the makers building to this specification) has built 90 variations.

There again, it is much harder for anyone to enforce standards for, say, all the city buses in Germany, than it is for one operator (however large) to adopt a particular standard and then rigidly adhere to it.

The main idea of standardisation is, of course, to save money. Fewer designs mean higher production of those which remain and the higher the production the lower the cost per unit. Standardisation should also save money on repairs and maintenance: fewer parts need to be kept in the stores, their fit should be guaranteed, and the maintenance staff should soon become proficient (and therefore quick) in handling and fitting them.

That such a utopia has so far failed to come to pass in the bus world is largely because the required volume of new vehicles needed each year in most countries (with the exception of America) has been too few to justify the mass production methods used in making cars. And if vehicles are being built by hand, or by relatively labour-intensive methods, there is no great financial incentive towards standardisation.

Standardisation has definite disadvantages. For every frivolous whim of a transport manager which has been stifled by standardisation, there may be a genius of a transport man with worthwhile ideas which have failed to reach fruition. If introducing standard

The beginnings of the postwar scene came in the late 1930s, when ST1140, alias RT1, was designed and built. RT1's body still survives, mounted on a postwar RT chassis, and in use as an engineer's instruction bus. It is seen here, centre, at Wood Green, alongside a top-number-box postwar RT and a small Guy (GS type) used for a time as a service vehicle.

designs is hard, having the courage to stop them and to introduce improvements is harder. If you are going to have a standard at all, you must learn to keep it for a reasonable time: yet this can lead to the perpetuation of old-fashioned ideas, such as the dated conventional lighting still fitted to the last London Transport Routemasters built in the mid-1960s.

At a time when there is all this discussion about standardisation it is perhaps appropriate to look at the buying policies of London Transport, past and present. Standardisation began very early, before World War 1 with the London General Omnibus Company's B-type, and continued with K of 1919, the S of 1920, the NS of 1923, and the ST and LT of 1929–30. London Transport continued with STLs, the ultimate in standardisation in the shape of the RT, and more recently the RM.

Mechanically some of these designs have had much in common with similar vehicles supplied to other undertakings: there has always been a degree of standardisation with the chassis and engine units. The problems come with the body which in many respects is a much more complicated structure. The LGOC recognised this with its body float: with standard types of bus 103 bodies were built for every 100 chassis and this body float enabled complete vehicle overhauls to take only as long as chassis overhauls: instead of waiting for the body, each finished chassis was fitted with a body from the float.

The system helped to give another dimension to London buses for the enthusiast as different types of ST, LT and STL body were gloriously mixed on early and later type chassis. It also gave an unexpected bonus to London Transport in World War 2 in providing a source of supply of spare bodies when proper overhauls and the float system had to be abandoned. The float still survives today in half-hearted fashion in that when a programme of Routemaster overhauls is undertaken, a number of "bodies" are used to create a temporary float which speeds up the return to service of the majority of overhauled vehicles.

The war taught LT other things. It was closely involved with other concerns in the London area in the production and assembly of Halifax bomber aircraft, for which specialised assembly methods were used, with much reliance on gauges and jigs to ensure that individual parts were within certain tolerances.

From this was born the postwar RT type, surely a milestone in bus design. Look today on the streets of London and see these vehicles still running in numbers—the newest some 19 years old. Any operator sufficiently determined can of course continue to run old buses (Paris used to be evidence of this). The point about the RT is that neither passengers nor crews find it dated and it can still be used in the thick of heavy traffic. One must salute the vision of those who in the late 1930s created the basis of such a design with its air-operated preselector gearbox and other advanced features. When I first saw RT bodies being built, at Park Royal in 1948, they were under construction alongside Dennis Lancets for East Kent, and we all know how old-fashioned and dated those look today—at least one is preserved.

To revert to the RT, the chaos of war and its aftermath created the conditions in which the intake of a vast new bus fleet was necessary and this helped justify the vast amount of design work and planning by LT and its two main body contractors, Weymanns and Park Royal that went in particular into the body structure.

Thus the body was designed from the very beginning and the tolerances that could be given to each and every part were calculated. More than 3,000 different drawings were prepared and the bodybuilders had to tool-up the job rather like chassis makers do.

The preparatory work was so expensive that it was only justified by a long and continuous production run. What emerged was a body which was a cross between the all-metal and the composite: it contained more timber than a metal body (mainly to ease the attachment of panels and floor boards) yet much less wood than a timber framed body.

Actual production was slow at first: it was

the middle of 1947 before the first vehicle—Weymann-bodied RT402—appeared but within 18 months deliveries had risen to almost a flood: by the Earls Court Show of 1948 (the first postwar one) Park Royal were showing RT 852 (with minor design modifications), having built RT 152–401; and 657 onwards. In addition Cravens of Sheffield were to provide 120 of their standard design, mounted on an RT chassis and looking similar to the LT-designed product, while Saunders provided an eventual 300 rather more like the standard LT design. Also disguised to look similar were 500 Leyland-bodied ones, which were 8 ft wide and mounted on Leyland chassis: the standard RT body was also mounted on over 1,500 7 ft 6 in Leyland chassis which were built to the same layout and dimensional tolerances as the AECs.

So enthusiastic did LT get for its RT family, which quickly showed its reliability and ease of maintenance, that they went ahead with a —at least in retrospect—slightly mad scheme to rebuild and rebend 300 prewar AEC Regent STL-type chassis to also accept RT bodies.

The first of these was SRT946, bodied by Park Royal with the body that would have gone on RT946: before the bus entered service it was renumbered SRT1, and in the end only 160 were built. They gave early troubles, mainly no doubt because drivers expected RT-type performance and, of course, the SRT was still genuine STL, small engine and conventional brakes included, underneath it all. After quite a few had entered service, they were all temporarily withdrawn and Palmers Green and other SRT haunts became filled with a surprising collection of old STs and STLs and certain new green RTs were temporarily diverted to the central area.

Most of the SRTs found their way to outer suburban routes rather than inner London ones and the chassis were eventually scrapped and the bodies remounted on almost the last RT chassis to be delivered. Although the SRTs had the STL type manually operated preselector gearbox, on them it was worked by an RT-type column change. A notice on the top of the selector box warned of the difference: stand up behind the front offside bulkhead on an RT and you can occasionally still see this notice, painted over, because when the SRT chassis were scrapped, the little RT bits they had acquired were retained for spares.

The SRTs and the ever continuing delivery of new RTs highlighted another snag with standardisation: you have to take a calculated guess about the future and you can be wrong. In retrospect it seems surprising, but practically no one in London Transport, or in the bus business in general, seemed to anticipate the effects of a rising standard of living, the ending of petrol rationing and the like. So LT found itself with too many buses and some of the last RTs to be delivered went straight into store. All the Craven-bodied ones were sold, and a selection of standard RTs went too. At first thought it would seem sensible to sell the oldest vehicles, but this would later have created chaos at the overhaul works: to keep even the future workload, you have to sell almost the same number of buses from each year's deliveries, otherwise there could be times when Aldenham was almost idle and these gaps would go on occurring every few years.

RMs were extensively tested before production began. Here RMs 1 and 2 (the latter then with small engine) are seen at Staines, where they were parked overnight while undergoing daytime trials at the Fighting Vehicle Research and Development Establishment track at Chobham.

RM2393, one of many Routemasters lengthened during construction by the addition of a short centre bay to add eight more seats.

In fact the RT and its body proved so reliable and trouble-free that the planned overhaul periods were eventually doubled. Last Aldenham overhauls were carried out a few years ago, but in 1972 there was a local overhaul programme on chassis at several individual garages, to gain fresh Certificates of Fitness and a bit more life from some RTs, when expected deliveries of new double-deckers and the ticket equipment for them were delayed. This again emphasises the advantage of a standard fleet: it is fairly easily possible to prolong its life. LT also bought 37 RTs from the by then separated London Country Bus Services, repainted them and put them into service from several garages, often on Central London routes, despite the higher back axle ratio that these country RTs had.

The successor to the RT was, again, an LT-designed vehicle, the Routemaster, which carried on the lessons of the RT (and also of a single "prefabricated" body structure built postwar on STL2477). The RM family were all metal, or all alloy to be precise, and designed initially to seat 64 and weigh, laden, the same as a 56-seat laden RT. Strangely perhaps, the RM has not earned quite the accolade that the RT achieved. Nevertheless the vehicle was again in many ways in advance of its time, though this was not fully realised in the 1960s. Although the RM was mainly an LT design (though some mechanical parts have an affinity with other AEC designs of the time), two batches were taken by the Northern General Transport Co. Ltd.

At this time the habit of salting roads in winter was not widespread or heavy: today it is. The aluminium-alloy structure of the RM is more or less unaffected by salt, whereas conventional steel body-framing corrodes badly. In the early 1970s, NGT—which operates in an area where the tonnage of salt spread per mile is very high—calculated that an overhaul for recertification on an RM cost it about £700, whereas the Leyland Atlantean or Daimler Fleetline cost over £2,000. It goes without saying, perhaps, that RM reliability is above average, though in LT service not so reliable as an RT: the RM

Mixture of the early 1970s at West Croydon. The London Transport XA Atlanteans were sold to Hong Kong this year and replaced by Park Royal Fleetlines very similar to the one on the right.

is a more complex vehicle with power steering and hydraulic brakes.

Salient points of the RM are a body structure that is also the main load-carrying unit, with small sub frames for mechanical units at front and rear. The driver's cab and front nearside is carried by the front bulkhead, while rear platform and staircase are suspended from the upper saloon. Stress panelling is fitted internally on the lower deck, but externally on the upper deck. Absence of a conventional chassis frame and leaf springs permits the engine to be offset.

The RM was followed by a rear-engined prototype, FRM1, which incorporated what LT hoped was the best of the RM design with improvements on rear-engined designs of the time. The main body structure was again built by Park Royal, and AEC was to offer the design generally. Plans were for an LT example and a demonstrator in Sheffield Corporation colours to be shown at the 1966 Earls Court exhibition. One or two other operators were known to be seriously interested—by this time the shortcomings of rear-engined double-deckers were being realised by their users.

Unfortunately the take-over of AEC by Leyland and a most unfortunate change in LT policy combined to kill the project completely. Now, in a modified form, the bus is being revived so that when Leyland's new double-decker comes along, with alloy body structure, and RM-type hydraulic brakes among other things, it will owe more than a little to the original thought of LT ten years previously.

Since then of course LT has bought "standard" vehicles from the bus industry though each succeeding batch is a little less standard than the last. It is always a nice story, by any bus concern, that its operating conditions are more arduous than those generally encountered. It is also one of those assumptions that is difficult to prove or disprove, and I, at least, had always been frankly dubious about LT's claims.

Unfortunately, LT are right—for me the point was proved by the use of some of the batch of 50 Leyland Atlanteans bought in 1965/1966 on the 76, a route that passed my office door. When you actually encounter broken-down buses regularly rather than occasionally the point begins to go home, and at their worst the Atlanteans were only doing 11,900 miles per failure, a failure rate over four times worse than that of the RT, the youngest of which were then 11 years old.

Probably both British Leyland and LT have learnt their lesson. Certainly it would seem that once the 2,000-odd Daimler Fleetlines on order are delivered, LT will make doubly sure that whatever else it buys is truly reliable and durable. Equally British Leyland appears to appreciate that some urban bus operating conditions are very ardous, and perhaps spurred on by competition from Metro-Scania, who have succeeded in selling large numbers of double-deckers straight from the drawing board, will no doubt get its designs right.

Meanwhile LT will probably mark time in the double-deck field—there's plenty of life left in RMs—and augment its fleet of relatively standard AEC Merlins or Swifts with Leyland Nationals or Metro-Scanias. For it has another ageing standard fleet not so far discussed—the RF type, based on AEC Regal IV chassis.

In a way the RF when new demonstrated the dangers of standardisation: the vehicles built (there were 700 plus, originally) came toward the end of the first era of underfloor-engined chassis and were heavyweights with a heavy fuel consumption. If LT had waited a year or two it could have had the second generation underfloors, the Tiger Cubs or Reliances, a ton or two lighter, and a much less voracious appetite for fuel.

In retrospect, it is just as well that they did not. The early lightweights were not overwhelmingly successful or long-lived in most fleets, and fuel consumption does not represent the same importance in running costs now that it did ten years or so ago. For the RF has proved beyond doubt its reliability —some of those with London Country are near the two-million mile mark. Furthermore, Green Line RFs ran with LC into 1973 still on Green Line service, though in their old

Few undertakings can have uprated engine performance and output on fairly elderly vehicles. RF47 is one so treated for the tightly-timed limited-stop Crawley-Luton Green Line service. The vehicles were downseated and luggage racks added at the rear, a feature that was responsible for them being gathered together again when a second route, 727, was also diverted to serve London Airport. The vehicle is seen at the Staines garage terminus.

age not achieving the 72,000 miles per failure figure of their heyday. But they do demonstrate the old adage that care in design and maintenance pays off: when LT refurbished them and Misha Black and his team revamped their appearance in 1966, the job was throughly done, with for example, new subframing beneath the polished aluminium strips which edged the deep light green stripe below window level.

LT also demonstrated the versatility of such vehicles by boring out the engines and raising maximum revs by about 200 on a batch which it lent to BEA for temporary use as executive express coaches between West London Air Terminal and the tarmac at London Airport: the vehicles were also fitted with spark arrestors.

Similar mechanical uprating and the addition of luggage racks and a larger fuel tank (the 35-gallon one standard was not large enough for a full day's work) was carried out on a number of RF coaches for use on the new 727 Green Line, a limited stop Luton-Crawley service linking the two London airports, and these same vehicles reappeared on that service when the RC-class (11-litre engined AEC Reliances) proved unreliable even after modication. Later the first RPs (later Reliances ordered by the now-separate London Country) displaced the uprated RFs, which staged another comeback when Green Line 724 was diverted to serve London Airport.

LT has overhauled a number of its central bus RFs in 1972 so it looks as if they too will be with us for a few more years yet. In the end operator-designed standard buses in large batches prove their worth.

In Between

Midi-bus photographs by STEWART J. BROWN

106

Facing page, upper: Art nouveau? A Morris Commercial with Ormac body of McLachlan of Tayvallich.

Facing page, lower: Stag Garage, Lochgilphead operated this newer Morris Commercial, with Plaxton body.

Above: This Austin is perhaps a small midi-bus or an outsize mini-bus. In any case, it belonged to Campbell of Callander.

Below: MacBrayne operated seven of these Croft-bodied Thornycrofts. HGG 104 saw further service with Martin, Lesmahagow.

This Sutherland Transport Karrier started life as a mobile bank before becoming a feeder mail-bus between Rhiconich and Kinlochbervie.

Commers with Scottish Aviation bodies were popular in rural Scotland. This was the entire fleet of McMillan, Pirnmill, on the Isle of Arran, in the mid-1960s.

Great & Adam of Alyth operated this Bedford on their Glen Isla service. The McLennan body boasted a small roof rack reached by outside steps on the rear.

A rare combination—Thames Trader chassis and Bellhouse Hartwell body owned by Wilson, Carnwath. Its most striking feature was the huge curved rear window.

Bus Driver of the Year

Described by D. G. BOWEN, MCIT

For many years the Lorry Driver of the Year competition has held a prominent place in transport circles and it was a logical development that a Bus Driver competition should follow. In 1972 several new undertakings joined in, amongst them City of Cardiff Transport and West Monmouthshire Omnibus Board and these two undertakings joined neighbouring Gelligaer Urban District Council to create a South Wales elimination centre. This feature describes the working of an elimination centre to choose finalists for the main contest.

Any driver who has qualified for a ROSCO or ROSPA Safe Driving Award in the previous year is eligible to enter the competition provided that he (or she) is not involved in a blameworthy accident prior to the date of the contest. The drivers then enter an elimination process to decide who will take part in the local final. Firstly, competitors are observed on normal service driving and awarded penalty marks for breaches of the Highway Code or poor driving technique. The most successful drivers from this section pass on to the Passenger Comfort Test where they are again secretly observed and penalised for poor driving technique, infringement of psv law and neglecting the safety or comfort of passengers.

So it was, therefore, that 30 drivers from the three undertakings gathered at the Cardiff Sloper Road Garage on a bright September Sunday morning in 1972 to determine the three drivers from each operator to qualify for the national final.

Each contestant was then examined on their knowledge of the Highway Code, psv law and drivers' legislation before passing on to the vehicle inspection test where they were required to discover a series of faults on an East Lancs-bodied Leyland PD3A from the Cardiff fleet.

With the ordeal of the more technical tests over, the drivers were able to concentrate on the three driving tests laid out on the depot

Marshals check the distances from the kerb at the conclusion of test 3. The vehicle is an Alexander-bodied AEC Swift of City of Cardiff Transport.

Cups to be awarded to the winners stand alongside a Cardiff Guy with a driver negotiating test 3 in the background.

110

bus park. For the first test West Mon had supplied one of their Willowbrook-bodied Leyland Leopards (4: VAX 62H) and each driver had to drive the vehicle forward around several bollards and then reverse past the same obstacles stopping as near as possible to a rear gate.

Gelligaer UDC provided a Bristol VR with Northern Counties body (39: BTX 539J) for the second test whilst Cardiff supplied an AEC Swift with Alexander bodywork painted in the then experimental orange livery (524: MBO 524F) for the final test which simulated entering a layby and stopping parallel to the kerb.

On completion of the tests, each driver anxiously awaited the judges decision on which three drivers from each undertaking would take part in the national final at High Ercall, Shropshire. A West Mon driver took the main honours at Cardiff but this was not to be so at the national final when the team from St Helens swept the board. If the representatives of the South Wales undertakings have their way, 1973 may be very different!

Above: Gelligaer 39 (BTX 539J) a Bristol VR/Northern Counties passes between the cones under the scrutiny of the marshals.

Below: West Monmouthshire Leyland Leopard 4 (VAX 62H) at the start of test 1 with the defects test vehicle, Cardiff 402, on the right.

Buses and Birds

ROBERT E. JOWITT on popular pursuits

If you admit that the vast majority of buses look extraordinarily dull in photographs (quite apart from what they may or may not look like in reality) then you will readily agree that the photographs need something to liven them up.

What better than girls?

After all, these countless swinging dolly-bird secretaries and shop assistants and assorted other varieties of maidens/wenches/chicks/ what-have-you all go to work in the morning on buses and home in the evening on buses (except of course for the ones who have lifts in the bosses' cars), so that birds and buses are closely associated. It might possibly be argued that housewives going shopping and buses are closely associated, or labourers going labouring and buses are closely associated, or various other similar situations, but housewives and labourers lack the artistic appeal of swinging dolly-birds, or any of the appeal (you name it) of swinging dolly-birds, therefore it is surely the swinging dolly-birds which make the best ornaments to bus photographs.

Furthermore, it adds a much greater element of sport to the game. After all, anyone can photograph a common bus—or nearly anyone. . . . And a number of people can make quite a decent job of photographing a girl. But to put the two together is not so easy. Well, you could always, provided you had the cheek, say to some passing damsel: "Come and stand in front of this super AEC/ Park Royal Bridgemaster while I take a photograph of it," and so long as the damsel didn't take offence at being used as a foreground for an AEC/Park Royal Bridgemaster and so long as the AEC/Park Royal Bridgemaster didn't start off while she was being a foreground to it, you would have a picture of a bus and a dolly-bird; but your picture would have been no more difficult to obtain than would a shot of the bus by itself or the girl by herself. What is much more difficult and much more sporting is to take both

Swinging London: an RT and various hairstyles.

at once without either of them knowing, and still get a good result.

The first problem is to find the girls and the buses together in the same place at the same time. So often does a lovely girl come slowly, photogenically along the pavement while the road remains quite empty, and then as soon as she has gone and the pavement is empty, a dozen buses come in quick succession, hastening furiously to be gone before the next girl comes. Or there are towns like Arles, in France, noted throughout the ages for the legendary beauty of the girls; a legend which still holds good, and incredibly lovely girls swarm all over the place, but the town possesses only about three buses which slink furtively along a very shady avenue. Or Winchester, where some highly-suitable-to-be-photographed-in-front-of-buses girls emerge from an office at about one minute past one, invariably, just after King Alfred's most attractive Leyland Tiger Cub has passed their door at two minutes before one.

And even if the bus and the girl are there simultaneously, the bus will probably be lurching violently and moving at an excessive speed and have telegraph poles sticking up behind it and cyclists and cars all round it, and the girl will probably be scowling savagely because there's a bus in the way when she wants to cross the road and she's late for the office and she ran out of shillings for the meter in her bedsit this morning and had a row with her boyfriend last night and one of the other dolly-birds (perhaps the next one you're going to photograph if that lovely Leyland PD2 isn't held up at the lights and can never catch up with her) is wearing a smarter and highly enviable coat from Richard Shops or Chelsea Girl.

So the first girl is scowling about all this and looks awful when the photograph is printed, and the Leyland PD2 does get held up at the traffic lights and the girl with the enviable coat disappears into a shop to buy slimming crispbreads so she can continue wearing her enviable coat, and there you are back with the same situation, or rather lack of it: in other words, bus and no girl, with the result that you don't obtain a brilliant photograph of a girl with

Swinging London swinging off a 73.

113

an enviable coat in front of a PD2 at all.

Still, not every huntsman catches his fox, nor does every landed gent bring down his grouse, even though he has a grouse moor to bring it down on. And even the best fisherman will sometimes land a tiddler.

So also with girls and buses. The bus is perfectly posed, no obstructions making it look as if it had no wheels, no chimneys apparently growing out of its roof; and the girl is standing there in front of it, perfectly posed, waiting for her boyfriend . . . or perhaps not for her boyfriend, because the trouble is that she is absolutely hideous. Low be it spoken, but not all dolly-birds are as fabulously beautiful as they might be, and you find once again that you have wasted film.

There is, however, a solution to the problem of the ugly girl, if you realise in time that she is ugly; that is, take her from the back. The fronts of ugly girls are sometimes compared unfavourably with the backs of buses. The back of a bus is (perhaps not unreasonably, except in the case of an open-rear-platform Paris bus) regarded as one of the criteria of ugliness. But the back of an ugly girl can look quite tolerable in front of the front of a bus. It may be curious but it is quite true that girls who are hideous often look super from the back. The disappointment comes if you see them from the back first, with gorgeous masses of long hair, with shapely legs, and then discover that their faces are far otherwise than the rear view promised. With buses it is the other way round; as you go towards the front, matters generally improve.

But blessed are the beautiful birds who browse before the best buses. Just as the sportsman bags, with patience, his salmon or his grouse, so also, for he who waits, comes a time when some superb female slinks sexily past a bus which is such a good bus anyhow that it hardly needs a woman to improve its picture. It is moments such as these which make the game worth while. And even if the bus doesn't really need feminine additions in its photograph, it is doubtless all the better for it.

Bus and bikini in Bournemouth. (A Leyland converted in ugly fashion to an open topper; so perhaps its subsequent demise was not so sad.)

The front view of King Alfred's Tiger Cub (seen here at Winchester Broadway) is very attractive.

Who can say otherwise of the mini-dressed maiden?

115

This neat little creature with the tartan skirt in Pau (*top*) must surely be called Gigi. A really gorgeous creature in Lucerne (*right*). If attention can be diverted from her, a trolleybus will be observed in the background.

A study in Bilbao trousers (*above*), and a not very flattering reflection. A pert Parisienne (*below*), and Bohemians of the Boul' Rue Gay Lussac traffic lights. (Tragic historical note: this photo was taken in the last hour of daylight of open-back bus operation in Paris).

Coventry Camera

Photographs and commentary by T. W. MOORE

After celebrating its 62nd anniversary in March 1974, Coventry Corporation Transport will become another division of the West Midlands passenger transport executive. The pte will be taking over a fleet of some 330 buses; Daimlers represent 90% of the fleet.

Coventry Transport has always preferred to purchase bus chassis built in the city by local labour. This policy began in 1913 when orders were placed with Maudslay for the supply of the six buses that were to pioneer motor bus services in the city. By 1932 a total of 51 Maudslay single- and double-deckers had entered the fleet.

Even four Dennis buses purchased in 1932 were powered by locally-built White & Poppe engines.

The standard prewar bus however was the Daimler COA6 powered by an AEC engine, and in fact Coventry was the only operator to take this model. It certainly proved a successful combination.

The undertaking continued to specify the AEC-engined Daimler by eagerly accepting 47 wartime CWA6 models, before ordering 96 postwar CVA6s. After purchasing 58 Daimler CVD6s in single- and double-decker form in 1949-52, the undertaking turned to Gardner engines in 1955/56. Since then all Coventry's Daimlers have had this engine, save one CVD6 in 1959.

Various coachbuilders have been concerned with Coventry Transport; Hickman were the main suppliers in the 1920s, Brush Coachworks and Metro-Cammell contracted for the 1930s, whilst in postwar years Metro-Cammell built all the double-deckers up to 1963. Since then, Willowbrook, Park Royal, Eastern Coach Works and East Lancashire Coachbuilders have come into favour.

True, Coventry Transport has purchased other types of bus, but, since 1934 Daimlers have reigned supreme. Coventry can be justly proud of them.

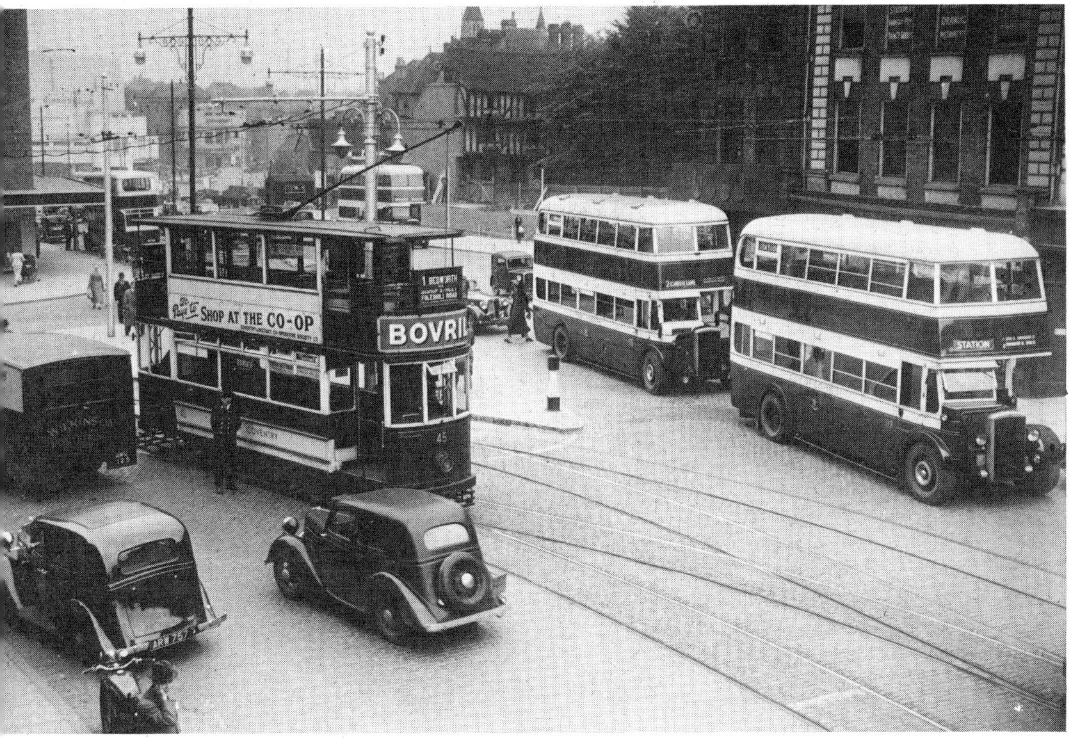

Above: Broadgate, Coventry 1938, and on the right Coventry's first oil-engined double-deck Daimler COA6 placed in service in 1934. Another Brush-bodied COA6 of 1935 is close behind, Tramcar 45 was one of the first purchased by CCT.

Facing page, upper: Coventry Transport's first motor buses were 34-seat open top Maudslays with 40hp Tyler engines but after only six months of service they were taken over by the war department.

Facing page, lower: Three 20-seat Brush-bodied Leyland Cub single-deckers were added to the Coventry fleet in January 1936, and 145 is pictured here in Allesley Village, returning to the city on the Brownshill Green service in 1937.

Right: Of the 21 Guy Arab Mark I buses received by Coventry, four had bodies built by Weymann for Manchester Corporation, but diverted to these Guys.

Above: The first postwar Daimler CVD6 with Metro-Cammell body in Foleshill Road in 1964.
Below: The last passenger chassis built at Maudslay's Parkside Works were nine 1950 Regents like 124, with Metro-Cammell bodies.

Lone Crossley GKV 100 was always painted in reversed livery and became known as "The White Lady" during its life. It originally was powered by a Crossley 8.5 litre engine and had an automatic gearbox.

A 1972 view of Daimler CVG6 289, then 13 years old, just after major overhaul and repaint to the new livery of cherry red/ivory. This is the type of bus that will be seeing service under the WMPTE ownership, as over 100 will still be in service at the takeover.

In January 1965, the 22 Leyland Atlanteans entered service, after a dispute over their size and increased seating capacity compared to the normal Coventry buses. They have Willowbrook 76-seat bodies and were Coventry's first rear-engined buses. They boasted a new livery and introduced a new destination indicator layout.

Loading in Broadgate, Coventry, on its first day in service, one of the 18 Daimler Fleetline "Monobuses" delivered in 1969. East Lancs constructed the attractive bodywork, designed for one-man operation, with a two door layout.

One of the three single-entrance ECW-bodied Bristol REs purchased in 1967, working the City-Railbus service in 1971, shortly after replacing Bedford VAS1s on this service.

Seek and You Will Find

A. J. FRANCIS looks at current trends

Typical of the buses used on dial-a-ride services, a Ford Transit with Strachans bodywork, seen here shortly before delivery to Denis Radio Taxis, Maidstone.

What you may ask? Passengers. The bus business is quite simple. It exists to move people, but in recent years the industry has fallen behind the race for custom, because it could not match the convenience of the private car. The conventional bus service cannot serve every customer on a door to door basis, and its frequency and speed does not suit everyone's need. Indeed, the cost of using public transport, although no doubt still cheaper than alternative means, rose by 62% between 1963 and 1970. Compare this with a rise of only 17% in the cost of new cars during the same period. Once a person has acquired a motor car, the comparatively marginal additional costs of running that vehicle are not a serious deterrent to making full use of this possession.

This is especially so when the private car provides, in almost every way, a better medium of transport than the ordinary bus. Congestion and inadequate parking facilities do not deter many from using the car. It is clear, nevertheless, that successful action must be taken if we are to prevent this natural desire from turning into a disease which will seriously affect normal life in urban areas.

Some startling statistics appear from the bus world. In the ten years prior to 1970, passenger journeys on local authority services fell by over 30%. On the other hand the car and taxi population doubled in the same decade. Where will it all end?

It is generally accepted that public transport must remain in the towns, but if people are to be persuaded to use it to an acceptable level, then the services must be to a standard comparable with the car. Let us see what is happening in the bus industry to achieve this result. We live in an era of experiments and these notes describe some which have come and gone and others which are still with us. Many are successful in meeting their set targets, some have lost their "experimental" or "here today, gone tomorrow" image and have become part of the normal bus scene.

New Towns

Many urban areas can date their road layouts back to the Romans, and others at least a century or two. Not surprisingly, these are not always ideal for today's needs. The new town building of the postwar period has created the opportunity to plan roads and buildings properly, and places like Stevenage originally allowed almost free use of the car. No account was taken of the phenomenal growth in the car population and improvements in the road system would continually be needed. It was thought that each year over £200,000 would be needed for highway construction compared with just over half that for a subsidised, but ideal, bus service. This was the crucial factor.

Blue Arrow and Superbus

With financial and technical assistance from the Stevenage Development Corporation and the government, experiments began in 1969. A reduction in private car movement during rush hours was the first aim, by providing a door-to-door service for workers between their homes in the Chells neighbourhood and the factory area. Blue Arrow was born—a personal taxi service using ordinary double-deckers, but distinguished by a special blue/silver colour scheme.

Tickets offered a guaranteed seat on specific journeys, organised so that buses served, as near as possible, the customers' homes and workplaces. Although many passengers were found already to be bus users, after a year, Blue Arrow claimed that a quarter of its traffic had previously used private transport.

This service was overshadowed by the more important series of developments which took place along the same route. Between Chells and Stevenage Town Centre the ordinary bus service (no. 809) was converted from crew to one-man operation, with the driver collecting fares and issuing tickets. On a busy route this did not prove popular, even though dual-doorway AEC Swifts were used. It proved an ideal route to revitalise.

In March 1971, the 809 received the "No Fuss Bus" with the same type of Swifts, but this time fitted with a farebox. Time was saved because no tickets or change were

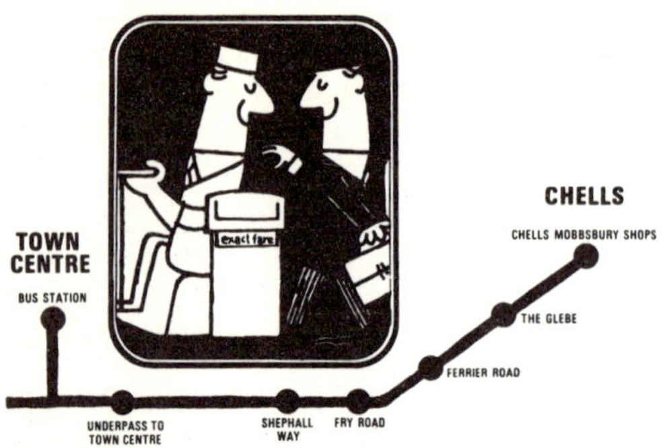

achieved, and one yardstick by which this success can be judged is the comment "Why can't the rest of Stevenage have a Superbus?" Well, this is being done, and the St Nicholas area has an almost identical service. On the statistical side, traffic has more than doubled on the Chells service since Superbus took over.

All this has been achieved with subsidies, but by offering a very high standard of public transport the cars can be kept away. Other new services elsewhere might eventually be self-supporting, but with many new town projects the important principle now is to provide a good service at the earliest opportunity—even before development justifies the high frequency.

Busway

This point was made abundantly clear at Runcorn where a twelve-mile road for the exclusive use of buses is in use. The new town has been designed to incorporate this rapid-transit system, where rubber tyres are employed rather than railed wheels. This road or Busway, as the whole concept has been dubbed, carves a figure eight in the town with the centre at the intersection.

Here, in addition to the shopping centre, there are easy links with the bus station for outlying areas. Residential communities are strung out along the Busway system meaning all homes are no more than five minutes from a bus stop. There is an ordinary road system for other traffic, but with Busway, public transport has a distinct advantage. Factory car parks are situated in less convenient positions than the corresponding bus stops and cars cannot reach every individual home. Because this means of transport cannot offer door-to-door convenience, the bus is not at a disadvantage and in many cases is superior. It is anticipated that half the journeys in the town will be made by bus, thus making the operation reasonably viable.

From the start, high frequencies have been provided with one-man single-deckers. Like Superbus, fareboxes are used to collect revenue, although unlike Superbus, a graduated scale of fares is applied. Nevertheless,

involved, but the graduated farescale stayed. Service intervals increased and a direct route taken to the town centre.

This particular phase lasted a short while before the new image Superbus was born in June of that year. Since Superbus took over there have been regular increases in frequency accompanied by decreases in fares. Added incentives such as prepaid tickets (sold widely), children's badges ("I'm a Superbus rider") and new types of bus such as the Metro-Scania single-decker and the Leyland National all helped to promote the service.

Success in selling the operation was

One of the Leyland National buses in the yellow/blue of Superbus, flanked on one side by one of the few remaining London Country RTs and on the other, a new Atlantean.

it is fast, and an approximate running speed of 20 mph is allowed for—an improvement on the average 12 mph for most traffic in built-up areas. In deciding that the bus was most suited for Runcorn, Professor Ling, original designer of Busway, studied other possible transport media.

Monorails were one idea which was discounted, as were various railed rapid transit systems. Another new development thinking along the same way is at Milton Keynes, near Bletchley. An extensive bus network, already started, is planned with strong liaison between the development corporation and NBC subsidiary United Counties. Every allowance is made for the private car, because it is accepted that on average 1·5 vehicles may eventually come to every family. The idea, as elsewhere, is to make people think of "hopping on a bus" as the natural thing to do. Adequate provision is to be made, using the bus, for the young, the old and all those others without "own account transport", to provide good services, and in turn to attract existing car users. Planners of

Milton Keynes put the emphasis on the use of small buses running at frequent intervals, although more conventional vehicles are being used on existing services.

The aim is to provide fast buses from the "local activity" centre, near people's homes, to their destination, followed again by a short walk. Once more we return to door-to-door convenience and a hybrid creature called "dial-a-ride", or a shared taxi, is trying to do just that.

Dial-a-Ride and others
Minibuses find themselves on a variety of tasks and at one time were considered, in some circles, as saviours of the rural scene. It now appears that they have entered urban transport in force. The dial-a-ride principle is claimed as a method of improving mobility within built-up areas by utilising minibuses on a high frequency door-to-door bus service. Such operations attempt to reduce car and taxi movements by offering public transport as convenient, reliable and comfortable as private transport. North America has popu-

Stevenage town centre with one of the AEC Swifts on the Superbus route to St Nicholas.

larised the facility and such services are surviving in areas where more conventional services may have found difficulty in finding support.

Those introduced in this country are services running from a town centre to residential areas. On "in town" journeys, passengers telephone a control point requesting transport and the bus then diverts to pick up customers at points as near to their homes as practicable. There is a basic route for the service with approved variations to work as required. Fixed stops are normally provided for those without telephones, or willing to wait, as the service generally runs to a form of timetable.

Returning from the town centre, customers go to the starting point of the service and give their destination to either driver or controller. A route is devised so that passengers are delivered, in correct order, to their homes. Radio control between vehicles and control centre is really necessary to maintain maximum flexibility. Eventually, if dial-a-ride were allowed to cover a complete town,

computer aid might be needed. It is argued that fixed route systems are not flexible enough to cope adequately with increasingly diffused travel requirements and the first to do something about it was City of Oxford, in Abingdon.

Every day, except Tuesday and Sunday, fixed circular routes are operated with a minibus to various parts of the town not previously served by public transport. But on the two other days, a dial-a-ride facility runs according to demand. A simple schedule is advertised giving the time of departure from either the centre or suburb of the town, allowing passengers to either "book" their journey by telephone or hail the bus en route. Fares are slightly above the ordinary minibus service, but well below ordinary taxi rates.

Shortly after this, a taxi proprietor, this time (Denis Radio Taxis) in Maidstone, began his own dial-a-ride from one of the railway stations to the nearby villages of Loose and Coxheath. This parallels conventional bus services but at the beginning, fare protection was offered. Not only does the

The picking up point at Maidstone East Station for the dial-a-ride service to Coxheath.

The **Leeds Shoppers Service** was worked, in the main, by Mercedes vehicles, such as 34 pictured here . . .

. . . but for a time, a Crompton Leyland Electricars battery electric bus ran over this route.

service connect with important trains, but also has a stop for the shopping centre. To attract traffic, this dial-a-ride introduced discount vouchers for the local shops and railway tickets. Unfortunately, the fare for the service was sufficiently high to discourage many from making use of the few advantages over the ordinary bus and serious attempts are being made to make the newcomer more attractive.

In the north, West Yorkshire put on a service with the fine-sounding title of Chauffeur Coach to serve, in the same way, areas of Harrogate which had been without buses. An attractive leaflet, which, incidently, served as a means of hailing the bus, detailed the areas served, together with the timetable and extent to which the service could be tailored to meet individual requests.

Giving dial-a-ride a name which will be remembered caused Eastbourne to dream up "Fonabus", and many other places, including Andover, Bristol, Guildford and Hampstead Garden Suburb are or may be trying out this novel arrangement. Areas likely to support a dial-a-ride are not those well served by existing public transport, but reasonably high class residential estates, where taxis are well patronised.

More ordinary minibuses have started in the capital where with financial assistance from the GLC, London Transport is running four well-used services with Ford Transit vehicles. These are timetabled in the same way as other routes but have a high flat fare (10p) to prevent overcrowding on a small bus. The Ford Transit is popular with all these routes, being employed on most dial-a-ride services, but in Leeds more interesting machines were used until recently on a shoppers service in the city centre. Modified Mercedes-Benz vehicles ran around the central area linking the central railway station, bus station and the main stores as well as providing transport in an otherwise pedestrian only precinct. The service started in November 1970 and in its time also employed an experimental battery electric bus, which has since been used in other towns on similar experimental services.

The limited capacity of minibuses may not prevent losses, as major costs are, as always, labour. Subsidies are sometimes acceptable as in the case of another method of wooing the motorist—park 'n' ride.

Park 'n' Ride
Leicester was one of the pioneers of the experiment in this country and achieved some success by offering the motorist a car park on the outskirts of the congested inner area and a quick bus ride for the remaining part of the journey into town. Christmas and Saturdays are the only time the operations pay for themselves unfortunately, but in 1971 25,000 people were carried, keeping 6,000 cars out of the centre. Costs of the operations are high and although other towns like Colchester, Birmingham and even London with its theatregoers' Starbus, indulged in the idea, a great deal has to be done before the motorist, after starting a journey by car, will be persuaded to leave it halfway. The saving in time, money or energy is seldom worth while, it seems.

Express Buses
An earlier attempt at "high class" market was made by Selnec, on the well advertised Hale Barns express. Luxury coaches collected passengers from outside their homes or at recognised stops in Hale Barns and drove them, complete with coffee, newspaper and a hostess, into the centre of Manchester. It broke new ground in offering an airline style of service, but earlier still Leeds had introduced a somewhat more orthodox express service from some estates, called Fastaway. Each was a means of raising bus standards.

Secure future
In the next decade we may see the return of the tram—or some form of electric light railway—as yet another mover of people. But the motor bus, in its ever-changing form, will be the mainstay of urban transport. After years languishing as a necessary evil, buses are now accepted as very much a part of our modern life.

Acknowledgements

Buses Annual relies on the willing co-operation
of the writers and photographers represented
in its pages. The photographs, other than
those credited in photo-features, are by:

AEC : 39
John Aldridge : 99, 101, 103, 105
G. H. F. Atkins : 18 (upper)
Gavin Booth : Cover, 41, 45, 46 (lower), 47, 86,
  87, 89, 90 (right), 91, 92
K. F. Cameron : 90 (left)
A. M. Davies : 64
Ford : 20 (upper), 124
A. J. Francis : 127, 128, 129
Guy : 19 (bottom)
W. Noel Jackson : 9, 13
Charles F. Klapper : 15
Charles F. Klapper Collection : 7, 10/11
D. A. Lawrence : 66
Leyland : 19 (top)
R. F. Mack : 42, 43, 46 (upper)
T. W. Moore : 2/3, 98, 102
Modern Transport Collection : 18 (lower), 19
  (centre), 20 (lower), 53, 85
A. Moyes : 65, 67, 69, 71, 72, 73
John Parke : 54, 55, 56, 57, 58, 59, 60, 61
Saro : 17
B. E. Speller : 130